The Compassionate Leader

How to Create the Space for an Inspiring Vibe

The Compassionate Leader

Jan Vermeiren

The Compassionate Leader: www.thecompassionateleader.org

Legal depot: D/2019/13.543/2
CIP Koninklijke Bibliotheek Albert I
NUR: 807, 808

Table of Contents

Introduction

Another book on leadership? That was exactly my thought when I started writing The Compassionate Leader. However, since I still see a lot of situations where people don't work well together, are not happy at work or don't reach their full potential, I felt that there is a need.

I also see a lot of leaders with good intentions, but who feel powerless because they don't understand what is going on in their team or don't have access to the right tools to support their team to go through change.

It is obvious that the current business environment faces many challenges. For example:
- The world is becoming more complex. How to deal with this evolution?
- People are looking for a workplace that not only provides an income but also offers the opportunity to put their talents to work.

Organizations, teams and people that are entirely in line with this have an inspiring vibe. They can achieve extraordinary results with fewer resources. They are able to attract and keep top talent, even if they can't offer the same remuneration. When people are in an inspiring vibe, there are also no restrictions to reach their full potential.

However, reaching that inspiring vibe is not as easy as it sounds. A company may offer a positive vibe — which is much more rewarding than a negative or neutral vibe — but still have a lot of untapped and often unknown growth potential.

To support people, teams and organizations to reach this inspiring vibe, Compassionate Leaders are needed. They are the facilitators to help their team or organization thrive. Compassionate Leaders are balanced leaders. They know when to focus on providing care for their team members and when to focus on stimulating them. As you will read in this book, both are necessary to move up to the inspiring vibe.

I often get asked the question of what inspired me to start the Compassionate Leader project, even before I started to write the book. Since the answer gives a good insight into my mission and drive, I'm happy to share it with you before we dive into the content of the book.

The seeds were planted several years ago with my previous company, Networking Coach. At that time, I was unaware of it, but when I look back now, I can see how it started.

To give you some background: we had a core team of four people and 12 free-lancers who worked with us at client projects regarding offline networking, referrals and how to use LinkedIn. We worked for more than 500 companies worldwide like 3M, Bridgestone, Bosch, Deloitte, IBM, ING, Nike, Philips, SAP, Siemens, and Swarovski. We were also the first official training partner of LinkedIn in the world. Something I'm still pretty proud of!

The initial observation was that some of our customer's teams applied our tips successfully, while other groups didn't get any results. It didn't make any sense when you consider that both teams had the same trainers, and 90 percent of the content was also the same. Since the teams that didn't get any results were not showing resistance to what we taught them, it wasn't obvious what was happening. Now I know. There was a difference in vibe. What that means, will become clear in the first chapter.

The second observation was that although the concept of self-steering organizations was not widely known at that time (at least not by me), I tried to set up a team that looked like it. I emphasize the word *attempt* because I didn't succeed. When I look back, I realize that I was the largest restriction, and we didn't have the tools to deal with tensions inside ourselves and sometimes also between us. In the past few years, it became even more clear to me that the vibe and consciousness level of the leader is a crucial factor. You will learn more about that in chapter 1 and 11. How to deal with tensions via the D.U.E.T. process will be explained in chapter 5.

This might be a good moment to admit that I've learned a lot since then. I'm not a perfect Compassionate Leader myself (yet). I'm still learning each day, like all of us. The reason why I'm sharing this is that you often get the impression from other books that the author is a 100 percent living example of what they write. This usually leads to a disappointment when you meet them and notice that they don't apply what they preach. The good news is that you don't have to be a perfect Compassionate Leader to get great results. Those results come step by step. The insights and techniques from this book will help you on this journey.

Besides the lessons I learned from Networking Coach, other experiences led to starting The Compassionate Leader and writing this book.

My wife Gwendolyn has a shop, called Het Vliegend Konijn, where she sells books, CDs, meditation cushions, yoga mats and other products that help people find peace, inspiration, and balance in their lives. Many of her customers work in large companies where one reorganization after another takes place. Most of them have a hard time keeping up with the changes or are in the recovery phase of burnout. It's heartbreaking to hear their stories and how they have suffered at work. Even more distressing is the fact that they take the stress and toxic atmosphere home (where they in turn 'infect' their family members and friends). It's such a loss of potential for themselves and for their employers.

On the other hand of the spectrum, I meet company owners and CEO's who want to support their employees to become 'the best version of themselves.' They know that purpose, autonomy, and mastery are important ingredients to reach that goal. However, just like I struggled myself, I see lots of well-meant initiatives failing. Although it makes my heart sing to see company owners try to create the best environment for the development of their employees, it's sad when they get stuck in the process.

After reflecting on those insights, it became clear that my mission in writing The Compassionate Leader was to create the space for an inspiring vibe.

Many companies take initiatives like using new software, redesigning office space, adopting new HR strategies, or other new ways of organizing themselves to reach an inspiring vibe.

However, most of those initiatives are focused on what I call *external* factors. While those external factors are needed, *internal* factors are overlooked. It's usually not on purpose. The simple reason is that only a few people are aware of them. In the meantime, 70 percent of change projects fail or don't achieve their goals (according to global management consultancy firm McKinsey & Company). That's why this book focuses on *internal* factors.

In the first instance, this book is written for leaders because they have the most impact on their organization or team. They need to be aware of what is going on and have the tools at their disposal to do it differently. But, I also wrote this book for coaches, change managers, HR business partners, project managers, and other facilitators. They are the ones that help the rest of the team or organization deal with the consequences of a leader's decisions (whether or not those leaders are compassionate). They are the ones who have to support leaders in both their personal growth and that of the company.

My intention with this book is to first give you insight into the most important internal factors that are usually overlooked. They are the differences in vibes (chapter 1), different kinds of tensions (chapter 2) and the attitude to deal with tensions and raise the vibe: compassion and Compassionate Leadership (chapter 3).

Then I will share a framework with techniques to transform tensions to reach the inspiring vibe: the four-step D.U.E.T. process. You will find an overview of the framework and techniques in chapter 5. Chapters 6, 7, 8, 9, and 10 will focus on different techniques and indicate which methods to apply in which circumstances.

Chapter 11 sums up the insights from the book, describing the habits of a Compassionate Leader and a pathway for those who want to become (an even greater) one.

When you apply the insights and techniques from this book, you will see that you and your team will find it much easier to deal with tensions and transform them. You will be able to implement change projects successfully.

My wish is that more people, in the first place CEOs, (change) managers, HR business partners, and coaches, become real Compassionate Leaders. We need them to create an environment where people can reach their full potential. We need them to create the space for an inspiring vibe for all of us.

From the heart,

Jan

PS: if you feel a connection with Compassionate Leadership, raising the vibe or supporting people to reach their full potential, even without having read the book yet, you are most welcome to join the free global Compassionate Leaders community where you can find like-minded people: www.thecompassionateleader.org

PPS: for readability's sake I often use "he" where there should be "he or she". Especially in Compassionate Leadership the gender of a person doesn't matter, but how he or she approaches life.

Chapter 1

Vibes

People, teams, and organizations can be in different vibes. To explore what vibes may resemble, let's look at four departments of the fictional company Gizmo Objects Inc.

It's on Monday. Ariane reluctantly dresses for work.

"It's good that my job provides me with money so I can pay my bills, but I'm already looking forward to the weekend. Five more days to go," she says to herself.

When she arrives at work in the customer service department, her colleague Nona takes her aside.

"Have you heard the latest rumors," she whispers. "One of our team might get fired."

This news hits Ariane hard. She feels a knot in her stomach.

"I hope it's not me," she thinks.

"Who do you think it will be?" Nona asks her.

"I hope it's Frank," answers Ariane. "He never does what I tell him to do. Or Christine, she always gives vague answers, so I always have to figure things out myself. Or Jason, he has been more at home due to sick leave than at work. But I wonder who will decide since our manager Hans doesn't have the courage to do that. Unless his wife commands him what to do, he is so afraid of her that he doesn't dare object." And she thinks: But to be sure that it's not going to be me, I will remind Hans of the flaws of the others.

A few minutes later, Hans walks into the office. Ariane asks him if she can help him. Hans is surprised because normally Ariane seeks ways out of any task she is asked to do.

"Nothing I can't think of right now, Ariane," says Hans. "But where is the customer satisfaction report?"

Creating a weekly customer satisfaction report is one of Ariane's responsibilities. Ariane answers that it isn't ready yet. When Hans reminds her that she agreed to have it ready by now, Ariane blames the IT department because the printer in the office is not working. When Hans tells her that there is another printer in the next room, Ariane answers that she doesn't have time to go there. Hans then goes to the other room, unplugs the printer and installs it next to Ariane's desk. Then he gives her detailed instructions regarding how to create the report and print it. Ariane reacts furiously.

"Do you think I don't know how to do my job? Don't belittle me like this. I'm not a child!"

Hans sighs and walks away. He has been pampering her and the rest of the department since he became their manager, but nothing much has changed in their attitude and results. No matter what he tries, there is still a lot of resistance, rage, complaining, and blaming going on.

Marketing specialist David is running behind on a task. He asks his colleague Thomas for help.

"I want to help," says Thomas, "but I have too much work myself. You have to ask someone else."

He looks around and sees that another colleague doesn't seem to be busy. She responds that she will help him, but that he has to wait until after lunch. David looks at the clock and sees it is three minutes before noon. "Yes, that is the habit of this team," he reminds himself. "Everybody is having lunch from noon to 1 p.m."

So, he stops working himself and joins his colleagues. During lunch, they talk about what they saw on television or read in the paper. At 12:55 p.m., everybody gets up to get back to work. While walking passed the bulletin board in the hallway, David notices that only half the department signed up for the yearly quiz coming up next Thursday evening.

"It's a pity that no more people participate," he says to himself.

Then he remembers last year's discussion. Most co-workers were enthusiastic, but when they heard it wasn't during office hours, a lot of them decided not to participate.

It is 1 p.m. Account manager James is preparing a presentation for a meeting with a client at the end of the day. He suddenly realizes he doesn't have all the information he needs. He calls his colleague Saskia for help. She asks him what kind of help he needs and when James answers that he needs the updated trend report for the IT industry by 2 p.m., Saskia responds that she doesn't know where to get it, but she knows that Gary was one of the team members who worked on it. James thanks Saskia and sends Gary a text message. He chooses to do it this way because, in their team meeting, Gary indicated that text messages were his primary communication medium. Gary responds immediately that he will e-mail the report. Five minutes later, James receives the e-mail, which allows him to update his presentation promptly. He is happy because the presentation will be ready in time to review it together with his manager Mandy. After reviewing the Powerpoint slides and topics, Mandy offers some tips including another layout option for the figures in the trend report.

Getting feedback from his boss is challenging for James. In comparison, Saskia's Powerpoint slides are impeccable, and Gary's presentation style is always tight and humorous. Although he dreads the feedback, James is always glad afterward. He knows it makes him perform better. This time is no exception. He feels confident that he will deliver a great presentation to the client. During the meeting with the client, it is clear that the figures from the trend report were the last bit of information that the client needed to decide to start the project. James shares this during the team meeting the next day and thanks Gary publicly for his contribution, Saskia for pointing out that Gary had this information and Mandy for her feedback. The rest of the team congratulates James. They celebrate success together.

Patricia and Daniel come back from their monthly Governance Meeting with the R&D team. It is the meeting where issues that influence the working of the team or organization are discussed. This time it was a different kind of meeting. Usually, they can deal with 20 topics in two hours using a specific process with consent decision-making. Consent means that proposals to change anything are accepted in the absence of objections. This way of working has helped the team a lot. There are no lengthy discussions anymore, and dominant people can no longer force a decision.

This new way of working had been one of the elements in the success of the team, and they have doubled their patent applications in the past two years. This way of meeting has also been a great relief because participants now gain energy instead of losing it.

However, today's meeting was different. Today, their colleague Jennifer said she had the feeling she had failed the team because she didn't deliver on her promises. Since it was clear that this was difficult for Jennifer, and since she presented herself from her most vulnerable side, time was created in the meeting to give attention to her feelings. Daniel volunteered to help Jennifer discover what was going on inside her. Jennifer agreed and went through the exercise the team used for this kind of situation. She discovered that there was a part of her that felt overly responsible and critical of her work. Other team members said that they recognized this part in themselves as well. It was clear that the mental obstruction in Jennifer wasn't leaving much space for the creative and innovative part. After Daniel supported Jennifer in balancing these two parts using another technique, the energy in the room changed. Not only did Jennifer feel lighter, but the whole group sensed the change that happened.

On their way back to their desk Patricia and Daniel share how grateful they are that they are part of a team where they are challenged to push their boundaries and at the same time invited to be present as a whole human being, with all their qualities and shadow sides. Moments like the one with Jennifer, help them grow as individuals and as a team. They don't have to hide anything. As a result, they can be fully focused on their job instead of wearing a mask to work.

These are examples from the fictitious company Gizmo Objects Inc. It's one company, four different departments, and four different energies. Maybe you recognize one or more of these situations in your organization. The larger an organization is, the higher the chances that there is a mix of those situations.

The Four Vibes

Those examples from Gizmo Objects Inc. show that there can be different energies in individuals, teams, and organizations. I call them *vibes*.

These are the four vibes:
- Negative vibe: Ariane's situation;
- Neutral vibe: David's situation;
- Positive vibe: James' situation;
- Inspiring vibe: Patricia and Daniel's situation.

Each vibe that is higher than the negative one is increasingly characterized by:
- Higher performance (efficiency, effectivity);
- Higher problem-solving capacities and speed;
- Better collaboration;
- More well-being;
- Attracting and keeping top talent (even with lower wages or fewer benefits);
- More openness to change.

The reason is that in each higher vibe, there is more safety, and team members feel supported to grow.

When the vibe of people or teams decreases, then:

- More time is spent looking out for potential (psychological) threats and less on actually working;
- More time is spent in discussions and actions as a means of protection;
- Projects slow down;
- Performance decreases;
- There is less availability of co-workers due to illnesses, burnout, or bore-out.
- Top talent leaves;
- Resistance to change increases.

The lower the vibe, the less safe people feel, and the less supported they feel in their personal growth (see figure below).

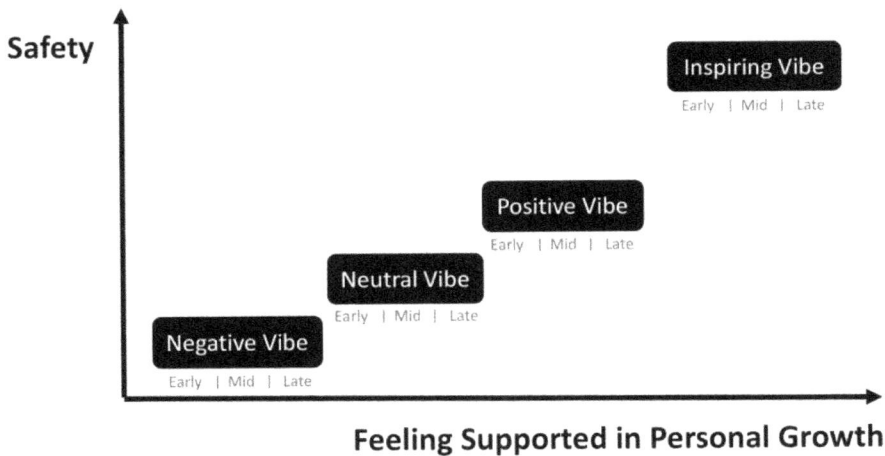

Feeling Supported in Personal Growth

The more people feel safe and secure, the less they have to put energy into protecting themselves or be on the lookout for potential danger. In most people's professional lives, it is not so much about physical danger, but about potential psychological threats. For example: "Is it safe for me to voice my ideas or concerns?"

The more people are stimulated to grow, the better they will perform, and the more they will feel supported. Growing can mean learning new skills or gaining knowledge, but it's also about becoming a better version of yourself. A version with less fears, more self-confidence, more self-awareness, and more compassion. This usually goes hand in hand with being happier and performing better.

It is clear that being in a higher vibe benefits both the individual and the organization.

It's important to note that vibes are not static but dynamic. Someone's vibe can change because of how they react to the circumstances. This change can be minor, which leads to a change within a vibe (which is represented by the terms 'early', 'mid' and 'late'). Or it can be a larger change causing people to move to a higher or lower vibe. Let's look at some examples.

> When a team with a neutral vibe is confronted with job insecurity due to decisions made in an overseas head office, the vibe may temporarily drop to a negative vibe level. When it is clear what is going to happen, the vibe can go to neutral again.

> Another example could relate to an individual or team attending a motivational seminar. The vibe can go up from neutral to positive. However, it commonly falls back to neutral after a couple of weeks because this vibe is not embedded in the working of the team.

Vibes can change. However, a dominant energy can usually be detected. It is the vibe that the individual or team is in most of the time. I call it the center of gravity.

In other words, the vibe of a person is the average of the vibes they go through. This is his center of gravity. The vibe of a team is the average of the centers of gravity of the vibes of team members. The vibe of an organization is the average of the centers of gravity of the vibes of the teams.

Let's take a closer look at each of the four vibes.

Negative Vibe

People in a negative vibe can be recognized by their **behavior.** They complain a lot, blame others behind their back and gossip. People in a negative vibe say they will do something, but afterward often don't follow through on their promises. There is a lot of (often irrational) resistance. Personal failures are covered up, and promises are broken. They have a lot of excuses and reasons why something can't be done. For people in a negative vibe, hoarding knowledge equals power. In other words, they hardly share any information, knowledge, or wisdom. They are also too afraid to share anything personal. They are focused on protecting themselves. The rules are bent or violated, if needed, to achieve that goal.

When it comes to **collaboration**, people in a negative vibe will only do this when it is forced upon them or necessary to protect themselves. They are reluctant to work together with new people or people who are different from them. Colleagues who are in another vibe are often sabotaged in some way.

When **change** happens, they are more focused on what can go wrong. This is because they are afraid they might lose something. They are focused on "what's in it for *me*," primarily to protect what they have.

When you look at their **availability**, they are absent both mentally and physically for a considerable amount of time. They take long toilet or smoke breaks. Absenteeism because of sick leave is also high, with potentially high costs for their employer. Mentally they are often not present. They spend a lot of time discussing worst-case scenarios, both in their head and with other people who are usually also in a negative vibe.

Their **feeling of safety** is very low. As a result, lots of time goes into protecting themselves from potential danger. This can be protective behavior when interacting with someone (like not cooperating in a meeting), but also being on the lookout where potential risk might be present (like hanging around water coolers a lot to pick up the latest news). It can also mean checking out social media during the day to make sure they are on top of anything negative that might happen.

Their **feeling of being supported** is also very low. Colleagues or managers are not available to help them — at least that's the perception of people in a negative vibe. Since their focus is on possible negative things that might happen, it becomes a self-fulfilling prophecy. If the glass is half full, they will perceive it as half empty and complain about it. Often people in a negative vibe are stuck in a negative vortex. This negative vibe usually repels people who are in another vibe, which leads to the self-fulfilling conclusion that nobody wants to help them. From an organizational point of view, the investment in people with a negative vibe is usually low. Only mandatory training is provided.

In a negative vibe, **feedback** is focused on what people do wrong. This contributes to the feeling of not being supported.

The **energy** in the office or work floor feels heavy and pessimistic. As a result, talented people won't come on board.

Neutral Vibe

The **behavior** of people in a neutral vibe is somewhat different from the negative vibe. Although the vibe is still low, it is not as toxic.

They still complain, gossip and blame others behind their back once in a while, but that is usually when they are in contact with people in a negative vibe. More than any other vibe, they adapt to the vibe of others. They do this to belong to the group. This gives them safety. The result is that they often put their own opinion aside if that is necessary to belong.

People in a neutral vibe usually follow through on their promises. They make sure that their work is done, but nothing more. They don't proactively seek better solutions or help out others when they have finished their tasks. Rules and formal agreements are their standards. That's what gives them a feeling of security.

Personal failures are still covered up, especially if they could lead to exclusion from the group. They share more information, knowledge, and wisdom than people in a negative vibe, but again with the underlying motive of being included or not being excluded. They are also not keen on sharing personal feelings, only superficial experiences like what they read in the paper or watched on television.

When it comes to **collaboration**, they tend to work together more than people in a negative vibe. The driver could be the need to be included, but also because they feel some kind of responsibility. They are still not very keen on working with people who are different, but they are less reluctant than people in a negative vibe.

When someone asks for help, they will first see if it fits their schedule. That can change if they feel they might be excluded by not helping. That's why they tend to proactively help people in some kind of power position, whether it's formal or informal, rather than one of their peers.

When **change** happens, they are more focused on what could go wrong, instead of the potential benefits of the new situation. They look for "what's in it for *me*" from the point of not being excluded and "what's in it for *us*" to protect the achievement of the (small) group they belong to.

People in a neutral vibe are more **available** than people in a negative vibe. They take regular breaks, and the rate of absenteeism due to sick leave is the average of the industry. However, mentally, they are not completely present. They're – unconsciously – still on the lookout for potential threats.

Their **feeling of safety** is medium. Still, a fair amount of time goes to protecting themselves from potential (psychological) danger, especially when the vibe can turn any time to negative.

Their **feeling of being supported** is also medium. They feel that they are supported by their colleagues and managers, but usually only when they proactively ask for it or when circumstances force it (like illnesses in the team). Organizations tend to offer more formal support to people in a neutral vibe than to people in a negative vibe. Initiatives that are taken by their employer include workshops to improve effectivity and efficiency, plus (often only superficial) team building events.

In a neutral vibe, **feedback** is focused on improving people's weaknesses. Their talents and positive qualities might also be mentioned, but the focus is on their flaws. The danger is that this might push them towards a negative vibe.

The **energy** in the office or work floor is neutral. It is not heavy or pessimistic, but also not positive or stimulating. Talented people might come on board but usually, leave the team or organization after a while.

Positive Vibe

When people are in a positive vibe, they are motivated to perform and open for feedback to increase their skills, abilities, and knowledge. Gossiping and blaming others behind their back doesn't happen too often. The reason is that they feel safer to address the underlying issues. They feel more secure, and their self-esteem is high enough.

They are less focused on protecting the current status quo and more on new opportunities which may present themselves. They are goal-oriented. This can be a personal goal, a team goal, or the purpose of the organization. They understand that to reach their objectives change is a necessary factor. However, sometimes, they are so focused on their personal or team goal that they lose sight of the purpose of the organization and don't take the impact on the ecosystem into account.

From the positive vibe on, people are more focused on **intrinsic motivation**. In his book *Drive*, author Dan Pink states that the three key components are purpose, mastery, and autonomy. The purpose is the feeling of doing something meaningful. It is the feeling that there is a relevant contribution. Mastery is the desire to improve. Someone who seeks mastery needs to attain it for its own sake. Autonomy is the need to direct your own life and work. To be fully motivated, you must be able to control what you do, when you do it, and who you do it with.

People in a positive vibe are not keen on failing or sharing personal errors. However, they know that addressing those errors could help them improve. Since their own development is more important than protecting themselves, they are willing to look at their mistakes, unhelpful behavior, or limiting patterns. However, the environment still needs to be safe enough. This usually means a one-on-one session with a manager, coach, or therapist. For deep introspection, when colleagues are present, a special setting is needed like an intensive team building weekend or a personal growth seminar. But even then, they only really open up to people they trust.

People in a positive vibe look for ways to **collaborate**. They know that sharing knowledge and information equals multiplying it. They are focused on team results and cheer each other on. They are focused on "what's in it for *me*" from the point of personal development and "what's in it for the *team*" to support achieving a bigger goal. The team can be their own team, but also the department or the whole organization. That's why they have a positive outlook on **change** and change projects. Rules and formal agreements are deemed necessary to have a framework to work in or to start from, but they can be changed if required after deliberation.

They are highly **available**. They take very short or no breaks during the day and take almost no sick leave.

Their **feeling of safety** is high. As a result, only a small portion of their time goes to protecting themselves. They are mentally and physically present at work most of the time.

Their **feeling of being supported** is also high. There is an emphasis on helping each other. Their manager acts as a coach, and proactively seeks a way to support their team. Internal or external coaches are also available to support team members in their personal growth. The organization further invests in these employees by providing a personal development plan and by organizing team-building initiatives that are focused on creating more self-awareness.

In a positive vibe, **feedback** is focused on how to strengthen talents and core qualities. While weaknesses might also be detected and improvements might be included in a development plan, the focus is on their strengths.

The **energy** in the office or work floor is positive and stimulating. Talented people are attracted to teams with a positive vibe. However, they will sometimes leave when they get a better job offer elsewhere. This might mean a better wage, more benefits, or the opportunity to work in an environment with an inspiring vibe.

Inspiring Vibe

People in an inspiring vibe are motivated and eager to perform and contribute. They are not only open to feedback to increase their skills, abilities, and knowledge, but are proactively looking for it. They know it benefits them and the organization.

They have a high level of self-esteem, but it is different from people in the positive vibe where it is often dominantly present. For people in the positive vibe, it often is a protection mechanism. It protects them from being confronted with their shadow side. In the inspiring vibe, people know that to grow as a person, these shadow sides need to be included. They **look for their blind spots** — and feel safe enough to do so together with the team. They know that in those shadows, the blocks are hidden that prevent functioning in an optimal and balanced way. Or the other way around, they know that the shadows can hide the greatest treasures for a rich and fulfilling life.

People in an inspiring vibe are **motivated** by contributing to a compelling purpose. That's why they can predominantly be found in startups or organizations that are focused on the greater good for the planet or humanity. Mastery and autonomy are essential.

They look for **continuous improvement** on all levels, for quantitative and qualitative growth, both as an individual and organization. That's why they constantly look for supportive technology and personal development tools and techniques. They know that rules and formal agreements need to change continuously to keep up with an ever-changing environment and have incorporated a safe and clear way of doing this in their daily work. They ask themselves questions like "How could I be wrong regarding this topic?" while in the other vibes people tend to defend their own ideas and opinions.

From a **collaboration** point of view, sharing information and knowledge is taken to the next level. Co-creation is embedded and highly stimulated. There is also a genuine interest in helping other people not only with ideas, suggestions, and practical solutions but also with discovering blocks and opportunities to grow as a person. They know that the process of assisting another person in embracing their shadow side is an enriching experience for them as well. That's why deep personal issues are shared frequently at work and not only in separate retreats or workshops. They are focused on "what is in it for the *ecosystem*" because they know everything is interconnected. They know that contributions to any involved stakeholder help to lift all parties, including themselves.

Contrary to what you might expect, they are less **available** than people in a positive vibe. They take more breaks during the day because they know it is necessary to recharge from time to time to keep functioning optimally. That's why they also take more time off from work to focus on activities, places, and people that fuel them in any way: physically, mentally, emotionally, or spiritually. That way, they prevent the specific kind of burnout from the positive vibe, which is related to working too hard.

Their **feeling of safety** is very high. As a result, almost no time is spent on protecting themselves. They are 100 percent present at work and show their vulnerability.

Their **feeling of being supported** is also very high. Since there is co-creation, they feel supported by their peers. Coaching by a manager or an internal or external coach is replaced by peer-to-peer coaching. Everybody has learned coaching skills because there's no time to wait for a coach or therapist. The organization is focused on enabling them to the fullest. The right technology, environment, and facilities are provided, together with a constant feedback loop on how to improve this support.

In an inspiring vibe, **feedback** is focused on enquiring how people can become a better version of themselves and asking what they need to accomplish it.

The **energy** in the office or work floor is exciting and energizing. As a result, top talent can't wait to be part of a team with an inspiring vibe. Moreover, they will stay, even when they receive offers with a larger wage or more benefits. If they decide to leave, whether it is to start their own company or to work for another team with an inspiring vibe, they will be the most fanatic ambassadors who can't wait to come to the yearly alumni event.

The Vibes on The Pyramid of Maslow

Another way of looking at the vibes is by using Maslow's Hierarchy of Human Needs - also called The Pyramid of Maslow - developed by psychological pioneer Abraham Maslow. Let's look at it with emphasis on the workplace.

Maslow's Hierarchy of Human Needs
with workplace examples

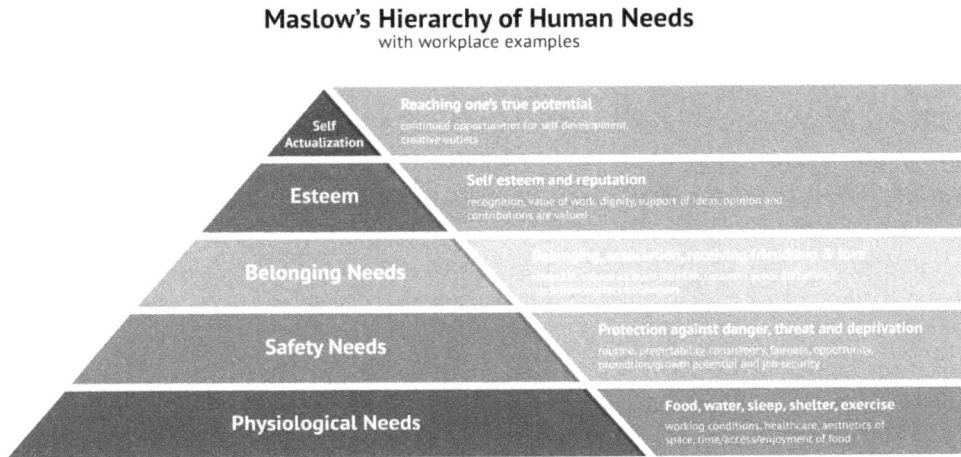

Self Actualization — Reaching one's true potential
continued opportunities for self development, creative outlets

Esteem — Self esteem and reputation
recognition, value of work, dignity, support of ideas, opinion and contributions are valued

Belonging Needs — Belonging, association, receiving friendship & love

Safety Needs — Protection against danger, threat and deprivation
routine, predictability, consistency, fairness, opportunity, promotion/growth potential and job security

Physiological Needs — Food, water, sleep, shelter, exercise
working conditions, healthcare, aesthetics of space, time/access/enjoyment of food

When people or teams are in a negative vibe in the workplace, they experience that their needs on one of the two bottom levels of Maslow's hierarchy (physiological or safety) are not satisfied or are in danger of not being satisfied anymore (for example, rumors about layoffs). The third level (belonging) is in reach, but the two top levels are not.

When co-workers are in a neutral vibe, usually the needs on the two bottom levels are satisfied. There is still a hesitance about belonging once in a while. For some people, esteem needs to start to play a role. The self-actualization level is not tapped into (yet).

For people in a positive vibe, the needs on the three bottom levels are satisfied most of the time. They are usually focused on building or experiencing some self-esteem. The self-actualization level is tapped into occasionally.

When people are in an inspiring vibe, the first four levels are satisfied. There are enough space, time, and attention for self-actualization.

Whether leaders are aware of Maslow's pyramid or not, many initiatives are taken in organizations to fulfill these needs. New technology, new ways of working, and new designs of office space all contribute to supporting people in moving up Maslow's Hierarchy of Needs. Most of these initiatives are focused on *external* factors. However, there is usually no attention to *internal* factors. For example, how safe people feel psychologically. The result is that most change projects are not as successful as they could be.

The Importance of Psychological Safety

In today's Western world, the basic needs (two bottom levels of Maslow's Hierarchy) are usually satisfied to a reasonable extent. The consequence is that today's main pain point is situated on the third level: the level of belonging.

This is a level that taps into most people's unconscious existential fear. When we were children, we needed other people to provide for us (parents, family, or foster care). For them to take care of us, most of us developed strategies to please them or not upset them in one way or the other.

Here are some examples.

> When Danny was a little boy, his father demanded that he kept quiet and didn't ask any questions. As a result, Danny learned that to be safe he needed to be quiet instead of following his natural tendency to ask for help or voice his opinion.

> When Joseph was a small child, he was beaten by his father. To survive (receive food and shelter), he let that happen instead of running away to be physically safe.

> When Nancy was six-years-old, her mother demanded that she help her. To be safe, Nancy complied instead of going out to play with other children.

We have learned to adapt to others in order to survive. This is usually an unconscious process that most people don't even remember when they are adults. This process is unconsciously triggered in the workplace in two main ways:
- Adapting one way or another to the group of people we work with;
- Protecting ourselves from the pain of past events.

Let's explore that a bit further.

Adapting to the Group Vibe

When people adapt to the group of people they work with, they usually synchronize their vibe level to the level of the group. That way, they can show that they are loyal to the group and deserve their place (instead of being expelled).

What does this look like in the workplace?

> A person who has a positive vibe suddenly starts to complain and gossip after working in a team with a negative vibe.

> Someone with a neutral vibe is more motivated to perform and starts to show genuine interest when working in a team with a positive vibe.

> A person with a positive vibe, who was a high achiever in the past, won't do more than necessary in a group with a neutral vibe.
> Someone with a positive vibe, who had a large need for individual recognition, becomes more open, vulnerable, and a real team player within a team with an inspiring vibe.

The stronger the vibe in the group and the stronger their desire to belong to the group, the more people will adapt to the group vibe. As you can see in the examples, this can cause an individual's vibe to increase or decrease.

Protecting Yourself

Every human being has encountered situations that were not safe. For some people, those experiences threatened their life (like war zones or physical abuse). For other people, it was more the perception that their life could be threatened. For many people, this internal fear has had a deeper impact than physical pain.

The result is that we have developed strategies and patterns that protect us. Most of the time they work unconsciously and steer our behavior without us giving it much thought.

The safer we feel in an environment, the less those strategies and patterns kick in. The more we perceive danger in any way, the more energy and time those strategies and patterns require. This is time and energy we don't have left for anything else. This means that we don't have the time and energy to do our work or contribute to the team or organization.

That is why it is so important to first provide psychological safety at work. This allows people to be in at least a neutral vibe. Then, for the organization or team leaders who want to create a positive and inspiring vibe, the second step is to provide an environment where those *protective* strategies and patterns can be transformed into *supportive* plans and patterns. You will learn throughout the book which tools and techniques you can use to create such an environment.

One of the lesser-known reasons why people leave a team or an organization or are expelled by a team is that they can't adapt (anymore) to the team vibe. It doesn't have anything to do with their professional skills, although a lack of performance is often used as a rational argument to fire someone.

If a person chooses to leave the organization, their protective pattern is to go to an environment that is safer or offers more opportunities for personal growth. This can be in a team with a vibe that is more like their own (a higher or lower vibe, up or down) or in another organization (out).

Here are a few examples of a mismatch between an individual and team vibe and indicators that they might leave soon:
- Negative team vibe: the individual doesn't participate in the blaming game (up or out);
- Neutral team vibe: the individual has more ambition (up or out) or complains a lot (down or out);
- Positive team vibe: the individual has less ambition (down or out) or needs more meaning (up or out);
- Inspiring team vibe: the individual finds deep personal development too confronting (down or out).

The primary focus of this book is to help people raise their vibe or that of their team. However, if that doesn't work out, it's also a valid option to part ways. When that's the only option left, my invitation is to do this compassionately.

How to Raise the Vibe of an Individual, Team or Organization

As you noticed in Maslow's Hierarchy of Human Needs, there are several factors in play to meet the needs of people within the workplace. For each vibe from neutral on, there are practical arrangements to be made to feel fully supported — like technology or agreements on how to work or communicate.

However, they will only be beneficial when it is clear what vibe the individual, team, or organization is in. Otherwise, they can even backfire!

The easiest way to detect which vibe is at play is to see what happens when tensions arise. These tensions can occur in day-to-day situations or in change projects. Change always includes one or more kinds of tension.

This is how each vibe perceives tension:
- In the negative vibe, tension is felt as a threat;
- In the neutral vibe, it is felt as uncomfortable;
- In the positive vibe, it is considered as a potential pointer to improvement;
- In the inspiring vibe, it is considered a crucial and indispensable factor for growth.

The stories at the beginning of this chapter show how this works. Customer service agent Ariane felt threatened, based on a rumor and is looking for ways to protect her position even when that means talking bad about other people. Marketing specialist Thomas is protecting himself from getting more work by not helping David. Account manager James saw the tension of a presentation as a learning opportunity. Researcher Jennifer was able to grow as a person because tension is considered a crucial factor for growth in her team.

In other words, the way people feel about tension depends on how safe they feel and how much they feel supported in their personal growth.

We can not only use these moments of tension to observe which vibe is at hand, but we can also use them as opportunities to raise the vibe. We can use these moments to offer safety and to support personal growth.

In the negative and neutral vibe, the focus is on providing enough safety and support, so people don't spiral downward when tensions arise.

In the positive and inspiring vibe, the focus is on stimulating people to grow. It is not only about acquiring new skills and knowledge; it is also about becoming a better version of yourself. It's about growing in consciousness and becoming a whole person or a balanced version of yourself. The latter is especially true in the inspiring vibe. It's about bringing your whole self to work instead of wearing your work mask (which is considered as protection in the negative and neutral vibe).

To be able to use moments of tension as opportunities to raise the vibe of an individual or team, a mix of several ingredients is needed for the leader or facilitator:

- A certain mindset or attitude: Compassionate Leadership;
- Insights in tensions, human behavior, and its underlying dynamics;
- Tools and techniques to solve tensions and transform their roots, which are gathered in the D.U.E.T. framework;
- Specific skills to interact with other people like Compassionate Communication.

These ingredients form the backbone of this book.

Individuals and teams in the inspiring vibe that have adopted peer-to-peer coaching also need to have these ingredients at their disposal, not only their manager or a person who acts as a facilitator. In other words, they are crucial for teams that truly want to be self-managing.

What You Also Need to Know about Vibes

Before we explore the attitude, insights, tools, and techniques that support raising the vibe of your team and organization in the next chapters, let's look at a few more things you need to know about vibes.

Going from One Vibe to the Next

Changing the center of gravity won't happen overnight. Jumping from a negative to inspiring vibe requires a considerable amount of time. But that doesn't have to be a problem. For most people, going up one vibe can already mean a lot. Even moving up inside a vibe can make a difference. For example, from early neutral (close to the negative vibe) to late neutral (close to the positive vibe), those people will be happier than before and will take fewer negative vibes home. For the organization, each higher vibe also means more energy available to do actual work (instead of spending time protecting oneself from psychological harm).

Although the inspiring vibe is the most supportive for individuals and the most constructive from an organizational point of view, each higher vibe above negative contributes to higher efficiency and effectivity. Celebrate each higher vibe and don't get too fixated on the inspiring one. In fact, organizations that focus too much on this vibe in change projects, tend to skip necessary steps and don't achieve their initial goal.

When going from one vibe to the next, you might lose some people. For example, when going from the negative to the neutral vibe, people who are deeply immersed in the negative vibe might not be able to adapt. On the other hand, you will probably also attract other people; people who are more related to the new vibe. However, when the vibe of the individual doesn't match for whatever reason, they will probably leave the team or organization.

This is why teams with a neutral vibe are sometimes able to attract new team members but are not able to keep them. The new individuals were probably on a higher vibe.

This also works the other way around. More and more organizations are exploring the concept of self-managing teams. Usually, those initiatives are situated in the positive or inspiring vibe. However, if team members aren't ready to make the transition to that higher vibe, the initiative will fail. Another situation can also arise. The new team member who was a high performer in another company, may leave a team with an inspiring vibe because he can't make the transition from the positive vibe to the inspiring one. He finds deep self-exploration too confronting.

Since the sum of the vibes of a team determines the vibe of the group (its center of gravity), the group might suddenly go from one vibe to the next when an individual leaves the group or when a new team member comes aboard. The smaller the team, the more impact the vibe has on an individual. This changing of vibe level is more likely to occur when the team is on one of the extremities of a vibe level. For example, when a new team member with a negative vibe enters a team of three co-workers in early neutral vibe, the team vibe will probably switch to the negative vibe. When a team member with a negative vibe leaves a team with the late neutral vibe, it can suddenly find itself in a positive vibe.

The Vibe of the Leader is of Major Importance

Research has shown that both the consciousness level and the vibe of the leader are crucial factors for the vibe of the team or organization.

But you probably don't need any research to know that. You've probably experienced a change in energy yourself when a new leader joined your organization, department, or team.

That's why there is much emphasis (in chapters 4 and 11) on the importance of a leader's personal development. There is even a suggestion on how to approach this: The Compassionate Leader Pathway.

As a side note: someone doesn't have to be a full-fledged Compassionate Leader and be immediately situated in the inspiring vibe. However, it is important to be one vibe higher than the current team vibe.

In other words, if a team is in a negative vibe, the leader should be in a neutral vibe to lift the team to a higher level. However, if the leader wants to increase the team's vibe further, he or she needs to raise their own vibe first.

The Inspiring Vibe is in Another League than the Positive Vibe

Many leaders think the vibe of their organization and team is the inspiring one. However, it usually is in the medium or late positive vibe.

Don't get me wrong; there is nothing wrong with a positive vibe. This might be a fantastic vibe to be in, especially when you were in a negative or neutral vibe a few months ago.

However, by not assessing the situation in the right way, the opportunity to reach the full potential of team members or the organization is overlooked.

In the inspiring vibe, it is about discovering the blind spots and shadow sides that keep us from reaching our full potential. These are aspects of ourselves we don't like to talk about, are ashamed of or frightened by. Although it is not easy to face them and requires courage to do so, this is where the biggest treasures are found.

Reflect on your situation: which vibe is the current center of gravity of your team or organization? When you think it is the inspiring one, compare yourself with the American investment firm Bridgewater Associates. Founder Ray Dalio summed up his company's philosophy in his book *Principles*. They include radical open-mindedness, radical transparency, making mistakes, and learning from mistakes. One of the ways Bridgewater implements this is to record all meetings on video. Even personal development sessions and meetings where people have a hard time facing their blind spots are recorded. This way, employees walk the talk: radical open-mindedness, radical transparency, and learning from mistakes so the whole organization can grow.

Although it's just one example, it shows what it means to have the ambition to be in the (late) inspiring vibe.

If you want to see if you are in the inspiring vibe, you can answer a few simple questions:
- Do I *feel safe* to share anything, even my shadow sides and events from the past that I am ashamed of?
- Am I *willing* to share my shadow sides?
- Is there *time and space* to share them?

If you want to check this for your team, put yourself in the shoes of one team member and feel how they would answer each question. Then put yourself in the shoes of another team member and so on. It is important to really feel what they would answer, not how you would like them to answer. This will give you a first impression whether or not your team is in the inspiring vibe. For most teams the answer is that they are not there yet.

My point is that it's not a case of spending too much time detecting shadow sides and transforming them, but that there is safety, willingness, time and space whenever it is necessary.

The benefit of being in the inspiring vibe is that hidden agendas and strategies of the ego (see chapter 4) are dealt with immediately. This removes friction from projects, from daily cooperation and from fulfilling the purpose.

I don't suggest every company takes the approach of immediately striving for the inspiring vibe. It is not advised to go there (yet) when the current center of gravity is in the negative or neutral vibe. It probably won't feel safe yet. Another prerequisite is that the leader of the organization must be in the inspiring vibe or have a heartfelt desire and willingness to get there. He or she needs to take steps to become an example, a beacon and a facilitator before the rest of the organization can follow.

That's what my ultimate goal of the Compassionate Leader project is: to support leaders and their organizations to reach their full potential. It won't only benefit them, but also the communities they are embedded in and all other stakeholders. When enough organizations are willing and able to do this, we will see the effects on a larger scale. Since we are globally connected via the internet, social media, and even physically (through affordable transportation), this can happen fast. It is necessary to solve global challenges.

Let this book be a source of inspiration on your journey. And let it be a journey. If your organization or team can make the transition from a negative to a neutral vibe or from a neutral to a positive vibe using the tools and techniques from this book, celebrate! Don't judge yourself if you are not in an inspiring vibe yet. That's already a first way of being compassionate. Celebrate every step along the way, even if it is just a baby step.

Key Take-Aways

There are four vibes in the workplace: negative, neutral, positive, and inspiring. The vibe depends on how safe people feel and how much they feel supported in their personal growth.

Each higher vibe than the negative one is characterized by:
- Higher performance (efficiency, effectivity);
- Higher problem-solving capacities and speed;
- Better collaboration;
- More well-being;
- Attracting and keeping top talent (even with lower wages or fewer benefits);
- More openness to change.

When the vibe of people or teams decreases:
- More time is spent looking out for potential (psychological) threats and less on actually working;
- More time is spent in discussions and actions as a means of protection;
- Projects slow down;
- Performance decreases;
- There is less availability of co-workers due to illnesses, burnout or bore-out;
- Top talent leaves;
- Resistance to change increases.

There is a link between vibes and Maslow's Hierarchy of Needs:
- People in the negative vibe worry about the two first levels: physiological and safety needs;
- People in the neutral vibe don't worry so much about the physiological and safety needs anymore, but they do worry about their belonging needs;

- People in a positive vibe feel much safer. They worry less and are focused on growing their self-esteem and reputation;
- People in an inspiring vibe have enough self-esteem. They focus on self-actualization.

Vibes fluctuate. That means that the same person can experience flashes of a negative, neutral, positive, and inspiring vibe in one day. However, their center of gravity is in one vibe. After experiencing other vibes, they come back to this one unless they are supported to raise their vibe permanently using one of the techniques of the D.U.E.T. process (see chapter 5).

Co-workers adapt their vibe to the group's vibe. In the negative and neutral vibe, they do this to protect themselves. This need for safety and security is usually underestimated in organizations. It is only when they are sufficiently fulfilled that people can grow to a positive vibe. That is the level where they start focusing more on reaching goals and collaborating effectively and efficiently.

Together with a level of consciousness, the vibe of the leader is of major importance. In most cases, that will be the ceiling for the rest of the team or organization. For a team to raise its vibe, the leader's vibe must rise first.

When leaders raise their vibe to inspire, they can create an inspiring vibe for the rest of the team or organization (which is in another league than the positive vibe).

Chapter 2

Tension as a Driver for Growth

We live in a VUCA world these days: a world that is characterized by Volatility, Uncertainty, Complexity, and Ambiguity. In a VUCA world, change is permanent.

In a professional environment, there is a saying that people resist change. I don't agree. The resistance comes from not knowing how to deal with the tension that comes with change. This makes them feel unsafe. That's why people resist change.

In chapter 5, I'll present the D.U.E.T. framework and offer tools and techniques to effectively deal with tension and transform them (which helps to increase the vibe). But before we go there, let's explore the different kinds of tensions in the workplace and a support mechanism to transform them — secure bases.

Tension in the Workplace

Let's go back to Gizmo Objects Inc. and look at a few examples of situations where tension is experienced.

> HR manager Jake and Chief Financial Officer Robert fight always. They don't agree on anything. When Jake was asked about Robert, he calls him a robot without a heart. When Robert was asked about Jake, he describes him as a difficult person who is constantly picking on him and always resists his suggestions. The tension between the two not only affects the atmosphere in the board room but has also spread to their departments. Whenever co-workers of the HR and finance department need to work together, they first have to present their findings to Jake and Robert before they can start executing them. This has slowed down operations. Many people in the company, even outside the HR and finance departments, describe it as difficult wade through mud instead of an easy walk in the park.

Account manager Jeffrey has had a couple of prolonged months acquiring new customers. Since this impacts his paycheck, he experiences a lot of stress. One day he storms into a meeting of the marketing team and shouts out: "Why are you giving me such lousy leads? I can't do anything with them! Can't you do your homework?"

Nona is an assistant in the customer service department. The majority of her work consists of inputting data from paper survey forms into a database on her computer. However, in the past three weeks she has been processing fewer forms than usual. Her manager Hans notices this. He also started to realize that at this pace, the deadline won't be met, which gives him stress. He asks Nona what's going on. She answers that her wrist hurts and that she needs to give it a rest every 20 minutes.

These are a few examples of common situations in the workplace where tension is experienced. Tension is felt a lot in the workplace. Since it's not a nice feeling, most people try to avoid it, ignore it, push it away, or project it on something or someone else.

However, when we do that, we miss opportunities. We miss opportunities to raise the vibe. We miss opportunities to grow as a person, as a team, as a department or as an organization.

Tension is pointing to something that is not in flow. When we change our perception of tension and consider it as a pointer to a deeper root or towards a solution instead of a problem, beneficial changes can happen.
Let's look at the examples again.

When Robert was asked when their relationship started to be so difficult, he couldn't remember. Jake, on the other hand, knew exactly the date and circumstances. There was an unexpected and urgent board meeting six years ago. It was on the afternoon of the day of his 10th wedding anniversary. To celebrate this event, Jake had booked a hard-to-get dinner table in a famous restaurant, months in advance. He had been looking forward to this evening ever since. During the meeting, Robert went deeper and deeper into the numbers of the company and asked every board member detailed questions regarding costs and budget. The result was that the meeting ran two hours longer than scheduled and Jake didn't make the dinner. He was very disappointed and blamed Robert. When Robert was presented with the facts, he also remembered the meeting because it was indeed an exceptional occasion. However, he didn't recall Jake mentioning anything about his 10th-anniversary dinner. He added that if he had been aware of the situation, he would have asked Jake about the numbers of the HR department first so Jake could have made the dinner. When Jake was asked about this, he admitted that he hadn't told Robert that he had booked that table.

When they both understood what the root of their conflict was, they were able to open up to each other and start cooperating again. As a result, things started to go smoothly again in the board room, between the HR and finance department, and through the rest of the company as well.

In this case, the tension between Jake and Robert pointed to a misunderstanding. Once that was cleared up, flow and growth were restored.

The background of Jeffrey's situation was that he received less than optimal leads from the marketing team. However, Jeffrey forgot that he had refused to give input for the creation of customer profiles. In a session with a coach, it appeared that this reminded him of receiving bad grades for his homework when he was a child. To avoid reliving the pain of 'bad grades' again, Jeffrey chose not to give input.

In this case, the tension that Jeffrey felt (small paycheck) was a pointer to pain from his childhood. When he was able to see this, he worked on this issue with a coach, delivered the input to the marketing team and was back on track acquiring new customers. The sales group was also glad because they felt that Jeffrey hadn't been part of the team. Usually, he was in a late neutral vibe, which was OK for the rest of the team, because the vibe difference with them was not that large. But lately, he had gone down to a negative vibe and seemed to get stuck there. It had had an impact on the rest of the team, but nobody had known how to deal with it.

This is what you may notice in many teams: good intentions, but no access to techniques on how to deal with tension. It can often lead to frustration, which creates added tension on top of the existing ones.

After a doctor's visit, Nona was diagnosed with RSI (Repetitive Strain Injury). Her wrist was resulting in severe pain because it remained in the same position day in day out. The advice was to try other kinds of work or find another job. Since her manager Hans didn't want to lose her (the team was already understaffed) he needed to find another solution. A few days later, scanners and OCR (Optical Character Recognition) software were installed. It relieved Nona and her colleagues of the dull, repetitive work of manually inputting the data.

In this case, tension (stress from the manager's deadline and the physical stress of RSI) pointed to an old way of working and opened the way for a more efficient process.

Not only can growth be restored or accelerated when tensions are solved, but it becomes a lot more fun to work together. When tensions are detected right away, they don't get the chance to branch out to other people or teams like in the example with Jeffrey. They also don't linger on for years — like in the example of Jake and Robert.

Dealing with tension not only restores working relationships, but it also leads to new opportunities.

Let's look at some examples.

Many customer service agents are under a lot of stress because they have to deal with unsatisfied customers. The customers are sometimes so frustrated that they first need to vent before they can even explain the problem. They need to get rid of their tension first. If customer service agents were better trained in compassionately deal with customer complaints, the outcome would result in less burnout and fewer resignations. Not only would they enjoy their work more, but they would also be able to detect patterns in complaints and log them. The company might be able to streamline their process better or detect the need for new products or services. Ideally, the customer service agents would be frequently updated about changes made based on their input. They would feel part of the company and appreciate the importance of their role.

An example from my own life goes back to August 2008. It was the moment that Groups were introduced on LinkedIn. Until that moment, LinkedIn was more like a directory of people. But from that moment on, interactions became possible. Networking Coach, my company at the time, had added several online business networks to the strategy of our clients besides offline networking. Until that moment, LinkedIn was third behind Ecademy and Xing. But that changed in August 2008. I felt positive tension and knew that major changes were going to happen. So, I bought every book that was available about LinkedIn. At the time, there weren't many. Any books available were focused on the buttons and links you could click on and weren't addressing the strategy and attitude that was necessary to be successful with LinkedIn. The result was to write my own book. It was a huge success: the book was an international bestseller and Networking Coach became LinkedIn's first official training partner.

Another example is the workplace messaging app called Slack. Not many people know that they were first a gaming company called Tiny Speck and created the massively multiplayer game Glitch. They shut down Glitch in 2012 and started to develop further the messaging tool they used internally. Because they addressed the tensions the company was experiencing, they were able to make the transition into a wildly successful business.

In other words, when a new perception on tension is embraced: that tension is a pointer instead of a problem, organizations might suddenly face a bright future. Conflicts can then be turned into growth opportunities and harmonious high performing teams can be created along the way.

Another way to shift the perception of tension is to look at the definition from Brian Robertson (author of *Holacracy: The New Management System for a Rapidly Changing World*). According to Robertson, "Tension is the feeling we get when we sense a gap between what is now and what could be."

When we perceive tension as a neutral fact that points out where the opportunities for growth are, working together reaches a new level.

Types of Tension in the Workplace

Tension in the workplace can occur in many forms.

When we want to use tension as a pointer towards the root or the cause, it is necessary to make a distinction between three categories of tension: practical or process tension, interpersonal tension, and personal tension.

Let's look at some examples.

Practical or process tension

Here are some cases of practical or process tension:

- E-mail is not accessible;
- Order and shipping operations are not optimally aligned;
- Data input is done manually and takes a long time;
- Co-workers are off sick frequently because of open doors or malfunctioning air-conditioning systems.

Process tension also relates to decision-making. When a decision needs to be made, one of these approaches is usually used:

- The manager decides whether or not having all the necessary information;
- Rules and procedures dictate what needs to be done without relevant questions being asked;
- There is a discussion with rational arguments, but the most dominant personalities make the decisions (regardless of their expertise). Introverted people rarely get a chance to contribute;
- Following a lengthy discussion where all voices are heard, the final decision takes all opinions, needs, and wants into account. However, the outcome is disappointing and uninspiring.

There is a good reason why each of these approaches is used. Usually, it's just the way that decisions have been made in the past, and nobody considered other ways.

However, most of the time those approaches don't take the underlying tensions into account. The way decisions are made can also cause added tension. The first two examples result in a feeling of powerlessness because individuals don't have any influence on the decisions impacting them. In the last two cases, there is a sense of frustration because of suboptimal solutions on the one hand and boring and time-consuming meetings on the other.

That's why I invite you to look at another way of decision making: consent. Consent decision-making is an approach where a proposal is made by people who are affected by the tension and is then accepted if there aren't any objections. The first benefit is that it starts from a current tension and doesn't add any extra tension in the decision-making process. It is also a fast way of making decisions. In my opinion, this is a very compassionate decision-making approach. That's why it is part of the D.U.E.T. framework to transform tensions. More specifically, it is included in the Compassionate Problem Solving technique (see chapter 7).

Personal tension

Here are some examples of personal tension:

- Stress: There are many examples of what causes stress. For a leader, it may relate to feeling the weight of responsibility.
- Feeling out of your comfort zone. This can happen on several levels, for example:
    - Knowledge: a CFO who needs to lead the IT department, but doesn't have any technical background;
    - Skills: giving a presentation for 100 Japanese people when you are not used to giving presentations outside your company and don't know anything about Japanese culture;
    - Emotions: receiving or giving a bad performance review.
- Inner struggle: An account manager facing an inner struggle between calling prospects and improving his sales presentation.
- Growth: The zone between two development levels can come with lots of personal tensions (examples are puberty for teenagers and a midlife crisis for adults).
- Health: Not being able to sleep well is a cause of short- and long-term tension.
- Goals: When an account manager sets a sales target and takes action, it may feel like he is pushing on the gas pedal and hitting the brake at the same time. Often, he feels guilty or ashamed as well.

Interpersonal tension

Some examples of interpersonal tension are:

- When someone asks for support but doesn't get it. Another example would be when a person offers support, but the support isn't accepted by his colleagues.
- In meetings, when a dominant person speaks, all the other participants remain silent or make themselves small or invisible.
- In the corridors or behind someone's back, people vent, complain, or gossip after feeling disadvantaged by someone else.

Summary of tensions

When we look back at the examples at the beginning of this chapter, the tension between HR manager Jake and CFO Robert was interpersonal. Account manager Jeffrey experienced personal tension and customer service assistant Nona faced a practical/process tension.

In short:
- **Practical or process tension** deals with something practical: **me and the task;**
- **Personal tension** is tension felt inside: **me and myself;**
- **Interpersonal tension** is tension with another person or a group of people: **me and the other.**

How We Deal with Tension

Since human beings don't like tension, the default response is to ignore it. That tends to be the strategy in the negative and neutral vibe and sometimes in the early and mid positive vibe. In the late positive and inspiring vibe, there's another take on tension, and it is welcomed as a driver for growth.

Since the center of gravity of most organizations is situated before the late positive vibe, the default strategy is to ignore tension. But ignoring tension doesn't make it go away. So, in order to deal with it, there are several coping strategies that are used, most of the time unconsciously. Let's look at a few that are used in the workplace, especially by leaders.

The first category is to get rid of the tension we may feel inside.
For example:

- Blaming someone else: the other is considered the cause of the tension;
- Venting some way: complaining or gossiping;
- Yelling or getting mad.

The second category is trying to manage the tension by going into control mode. For example:

- Micromanagement: continuously checking the work of others in a very detailed way;
- Enforce one's approach to others;
- Suppress the tension internally or take the blame.

A major drawback of this last strategy is that it often leads to physical or mental disorders like back pain, headaches, and burn out. As a consequence, a good way to take care of yourself is by not suppressing the tension. Since most people don't know how to do that, they use strategies of the first category. However, that usually comes with the cost of damaging relationships.

It doesn't matter which of the above strategies is used, the result is almost always that the connection with other people gets disrupted. When we start yelling at people, we push them away. Even when we suppress the tension internally or take the blame, the connection gets disrupted — we withdraw ourselves and become less available to others.

Since our own coping strategy is usually unknown to us — it is *unconscious* behavior — it feels that the disconnect we experience, is someone else's fault. The usual response is to blame or reject them. It makes the disconnection even larger and creates a new (interpersonal) tension.

The result is a decrease in productivity, efficiency, and effectivity. There is also a decrease in happiness and well-being both at work and at home. Even if someone's coping strategy is to yell, it might not happen at work because of the potential consequences. The place to yell is more commonly at home. However, this creates a new tension with family members. This new tension also needs a way out. In my opinion, this is one of the major reasons why so many people in the western world are unhappy in a time when living conditions have never been better.

Another example of ignoring tension is related to meetings. There is the phenomenon of the 'elephant in the room'. This is a topic that is present and has one or more kinds of tension attached to it. Everybody knows and feels its presence, but nobody addresses the topic. The longer the elephant is ignored, the more tension is built up, and the larger the elephant grows. By the time the issue is addressed, wrong decisions have been made, conflicts have erupted and relationships got damaged.

What makes human beings behave this way? There are several reasons, but one of the most important underlying ones is personal survival. Will we make the – often unconscious – decision to adapt to a group dynamic or not?

In this interconnected world, it is very rare to accomplish anything on our own anymore. Even for basic needs like food, most of us are dependent on a supply chain from farmer to distributor to shop. Whether we like it or not, we need to adapt to certain group rules. So even when we perceive tension within our group, voicing our displeasure could get us kicked out. In some African tribes, being expelled from the group still literally means death.

One of the differences between the lower vibes (negative and neutral) and the higher vibes (positive and inspiring) is the way tension is determined. In the higher vibes, tension is seen as positive. It is considered a gift for growth.

The good news is that there are other ways of dealing with tension, even for people in a negative vibe who perceive tension as a threat. There are ways of turning this situation around and even use tension as a way to grow as individuals, teams, and organizations. An essential first ingredient in this approach is the availability of secure bases (see below). The second ingredient is the Compassionate Leadership attitude (chapter 3). A third ingredient is the D.U.E.T. framework to transform tensions (chapter 5).

Secure Bases

In their book *Care to Dare,* authors George Kohlrieser, Susan Goldsworthy and Duncan Coombe describe the need for *secure bases*.

They define a *secure base* as a person, place, goal or object that provides a sense of protection, safety, and caring *and* offers a source of inspiration and energy for exploration, risk-taking, and challenges. The more secure and supported a person feels, the easier it is for them to look at tension.

To understand why we all need secure bases, consider how the human brain works. When an actual or perceived threat to survival emerges, the primal brain will prompt the individual to resist change or avoid risk as a means of protection. However, when the individual has a secure base, the focus changes from pain, anger, fear, and loss, to reward, opportunity, and benefit. In other words, the individual can make the transition from a lower vibe (negative or neutral) to a higher vibe (positive or inspiring).

The authors also add that while the strongest secure bases often take the form of people, secure bases can also be anything that shuts down the early warning system in the brain and provides the energy and inspiration to seek a challenge. Places, goals, and objects can be secure bases, as can a country, a religion, an event, a group or a pet. A secure base can be any entity that, through a relationship, enhances a person's inner sense of safety and inspires exploration. The stronger the secure base, the more resilient the person becomes in the face of adverse or stressful circumstances. Because the need for a secure base is rooted deep within the brain, the secure base concept applies universally across all cultures and generations.

If leaders want to support their teams to grow to a higher vibe, it's important to be a secure base for them and to help them find other secure bases as well.

Many leaders fear that to be a secure base they need to be available at all times. It turns out that physical proximity and frequency of interaction are less important than the *perceived* availability when support is needed.

However, it's not always that easy to be a secure base for others. That's why leaders need to create more inner safety and security first. This is done by looking at their shadow sides and transforming them (see chapter 4). It is also important to have secure bases for themselves. In order to perform well, everybody needs support. Leaders are no exception.

Being a secure base is part of Compassionate Leadership. You will find tips and techniques to create more inner safety and security throughout the book. Exercises on how to find secure bases can be found in the free section of the Training Center on the website.

The Impact of Tension on Leaders

Leaders belong to the category of people who come across lots of tensions.

This is most obvious when they experience personal tension. The traditional view is that a leader is supposed to know how to do deal with tension. Though it might not be the opinion of others, leaders often have the feeling that they should have all the solutions and be in control. This usually increases tension and stress.

This feeling is often present when tension arises in a team or an organization. The leader is usually expected to know what to do and to make the right decision. Again, this is not always the opinion of team members or employees. However, many leaders have a huge sense of responsibility. When tensions arise, and a leader can't solve them, they often feel powerless. For people with a huge sense of responsibility, this is even more difficult to handle. That's the first reason why leaders need techniques to solve tension and transform the root cause.

Whether or not leaders have a huge sense of responsibility, the tensions that arise in their team or organization have an impact on them. If it relates to *practical or process tension*, a practical solution is needed. Since most organizations are not self-managing, this usually involves some kind of input from the leader. If it's about *interpersonal tensions*, every team member, including the leader, feels it. Those tensions impact the atmosphere in the workplace and during meetings. It can decrease efficiency, effectivity, productivity and team spirit. If a team member experiences *personal tensions*, this has an effect on their performance and could be influencing other team members as well. In all those cases it is usually up to the leader to find some kind of solution.

The impact on a leader doesn't stop when tensions are perceived as negative. In the case of positive tensions, like new market opportunities or technological advances, the leader is usually involved or consulted about what (not) to do.

Whether tensions are perceived as negative or positive, they are experienced at the moment they arise. They are not planned. The consequence is that they have to be dealt with besides the normal day-to-day operations. The result is often that planned work needs to be taken home, which affects family and social life.

That's why leaders are the first ones to acquire techniques to transform tensions. The consequence of transforming tensions is that the vibe rises. This applies to individuals, teams, and organizations. And that's why the techniques to do this have a central place in this book. You will discover them from chapter 5 on, after exploring what compassion in the workplace and Compassionate Leadership is all about in chapter 3 and which elements block the raising of the vibe in chapter 4.

Key Take-Aways

Tensions are a part of the workplace. They can show up in day-to-day work and in moments of change.

There are three types of tension: practical or process tension, personal tension, and interpersonal tension.
- Practical or process tension is tension regarding something practical: me and the task.
- Personal tension is tension felt inside: me and myself.
- Interpersonal tension is tension with another person or a group of people: me and the other.

The default strategy for human beings experiencing tension is to avoid it, ignore it, or push it away.

In organizations, most tensions are related to practical or process tensions. However, if they are not dealt with, they can become interpersonal tensions and become mixed up with personal tensions as well.

Tension always seeks a way out. Strategies to get rid of tension are: blaming someone else, venting (complaining or gossiping) or getting mad. Strategies for trying to control tension are: micro-management, enforcing one's own way of working to others and suppressing tension internally.

Those latter strategies are used by leaders who don't have the right techniques and tools. Because of their role or their sense of responsibility, they usually have to deal with even more tensions than co-workers. But most of them don't know how to solve them properly.

When tensions are ignored, it affects the vibe of the individual or team nega-tively. That's why it's essential to have a good framework to process tensions in a healthy way.

One of the ingredients of this framework is the availability of secure bases that enhance people's inner sense of safety and inspire exploration. You will find tips and techniques to create more inner safety and security throughout the book. Exercises of how to find secure bases can be found in the Training Center on the website.

A second ingredient is the Compassionate Leadership attitude (see chapter 3). Another ingredient is the D.U.E.T. process to transform tensions (see chapter 5). Transforming tensions creates the space for the inspiring vibe.

Chapter 3

Compassionate Leadership

From the previous chapter, we know that secure bases are a helpful ingredient in transforming tensions into growth opportunities; and creating the space for an inspiring vibe.

In this chapter, we will look into another ingredient: Compassionate Leadership. But let's start with the concept of compassion itself.

Compassion

The word 'compassion' is often linked to suffering. While I tend to agree with that statement, I have a different view than most people. Let me explain.

The first key insight I want to share about compassion is that I make a distinction between pain and suffering.

For me, the difference between pain and suffering is that pain is a physical or emotional experience. Suffering is about identifying with the pain and clinging to it. Suffering usually relates to feeling like a victim, feeling disadvantaged or powerless. Suffering keeps people small and usually keeps them stuck in the past. When we feel pity for them, it only magnifies the problem and makes them even smaller.

Actually, every time we feel pity for someone — even if they don't consider themselves a victim — we put them in that situation of victimhood. Often, you might feel like a savior. Although there are usually good intentions behind it, taking on the role of savior turns the other person into a victim, even if they don't feel like one. That's one of the reasons why you sometimes receive a negative reaction when you offer to help someone. Since they don't want to be considered a victim, they would rather refuse your help. It's not you or your help being rejected, but the – unconscious – savior-victim pattern.

Making the distinction between pain and suffering is a first step in getting out of that situation. When people can acknowledge that something is painful or when they can feel the pain without identifying with it, they still have access to solutions and their strength. Since most people don't make that distinction, one aspect of being compassionate is to support them in noticing the difference between pain and suffering.

A second key insight can be found in the origins of the word. Compassion is the construction of two words: *com* and *passion*. *Com* means *with* and *passion* refers to *great emotion* or *suffering*. As a consequence, compassion is usually translated to *suffer with*.

Since compassion is at the heart of many religions, people embrace this concept as a way into heaven. Usually this results in people feeling sorry or feeling pity for someone else. They tell the other person or other people how terrible it is what they are going through. It's often a fake situation with no real emotional connection with the other person. Or the opposite can happen: some people turn to deeply feeling the emotions of other people. They experience the pain or suffering from the other person and often start suffering themselves. This deep feeling is what empaths or HSPs (Highly Sensitive People) often do.

For me, both examples are wrong interpretations of the word. For me, the translation is not *suffer with*, but *be with pain or suffering*.

This makes a huge difference, doesn't it?

Compassion is being able to be with someone without suffering yourself — even if they're having a hard time or behaving negatively. It's about seeing them as a fellow, equivalent human being, not as a victim. It is about being able to keep a focus on their talents and positive qualities, while allowing the pain to be expressed, no matter how small or large.

We all experience tensions in the workplace. Both small and large ones. It is clear that compassion is needed for the large ones. But even small tensions can slowly undermine a person until it turns into a large event like burnout. As a leader, it is important to also notice the small tensions your team members are struggling with and be with them in a compassionate way. Then techniques from the D.U.E.T. process (see chapter 5) can be used to solve those tensions.

To be clear: being compassionate doesn't mean tolerating negative behavior. It means noticing the behavior and knowing that it's a way of trying to get rid of tension. Being compassionate is being able first to allow the tension to be expressed in a non-destructive way. This is followed by discovering and, if possible, transforming the root of the tension. It's about knowing that tension is a symptom of what's really going on.

Being compassionate is about helping the other person get out of victim mode (if they were in it) and helping them to see other options. It's about staying in your own center, your personal power and not being sucked into another person's energy. It's about connecting with the other person, without getting caught up in their feelings and emotions. This allows you to be able to keep seeing new options.

After dealing with the person and their pain, you must decide whether or not to take action. If you decide to act, it needs to be confirmed with the other person. An action doesn't have to be a solution. An action can be as simple as asking a question, listening, referring the person to someone else or making a phone call. A big potential trap is to take the savior position. A savior position can disempower the other person, so refrain from doing it.

Last, but not least, as a leader it is important to have compassion for yourself. Self-compassion means applying the same concept personally: *be with your own suffering*. Then you can take the following steps: acknowledge the pain, separate the pain from the suffering and decide whether or not to act.

Compassionate Leadership

As you may have noticed, being compassionate with others is already a form of leadership. But to make it more applicable to the workplace, I have created a specific definition of Compassionate Leadership:

"The ability to take individuals, teams, and organizations to a higher vibe, meaning a higher level of performance and well-being, in a safe and stimulating way when tensions occur."

The definition of compassion is not explicitly present in this definition, but is implicitly embedded in the words "a safe and stimulating way when tensions occur." The concept of being a secure base is implicitly present as well.

Compassionate Leadership is about focusing on the talents and skills of your team members, especially when there are temporary setbacks. It's about supporting people out of victimhood and into their zone of genius. It's about stimulating co-workers to grow further.

Compassionate Leadership is about being a secure base when people are having a hard time or are vulnerable during their journey of introspection and self-discovery. It's about providing security and safety for your team, even when the situation doesn't feel secure (layoffs or a merger).

For people and teams in a negative or neutral vibe, the emphasis needs to be on providing safety and security. When those needs are not met, they are not open yet to discover their talents and they are not ready yet for personal development. That's why the focus needs to be on safety and security in the negative or neutral vibe.

For people and teams in a positive or inspiring vibe, the focus shifts to stimulating the development of talent and skill and facilitating self-discovery. They need to feel supported in their personal development.

Compassionate Leadership, this ability to take individuals, teams, and organizations to a higher level of performance and well-being in a safe and stimulating way when tensions occur, is present in everybody. In some people, it's already more developed than in others. The good news is that it can be cultivated and trained if necessary. One of the ways to do that is by following the Compassionate Leader Pathway (see chapter 11).

Compassionate Leadership is crucial when dealing with tensions and helping people and teams to raise their vibe. It is especially important in any change project or any change in general.

One of the reasons is that people need to be able to successfully go through a few steps before they can make the transition from an old to a new situation. This process usually includes tensions and a temporary decrease of the vibe. This is a natural process.

However, not many leaders are aware of this process. As a result, they don't give their team or organization space and time to go through those steps. The consequence is that they might get stuck in one of the steps, causing a permanent decrease in the center of gravity of the vibe of the team or organization. If the process is not dealt with compassionately, the vibe might even decrease further.

Since this process has such a profound impact, let's look at it in more detail.

The Bonding Cycle

The bonding cycle is a process that consists of four stages. Not being able to go through the bonding cycle is one of the main reasons why change projects (and any change in general) fail or are not as successful as they could be.

In their book *Care to Dare,* authors George Kohlrieser, Susan Goldsworthy and Duncan Coombe explain the four stages of the bonding cycle.

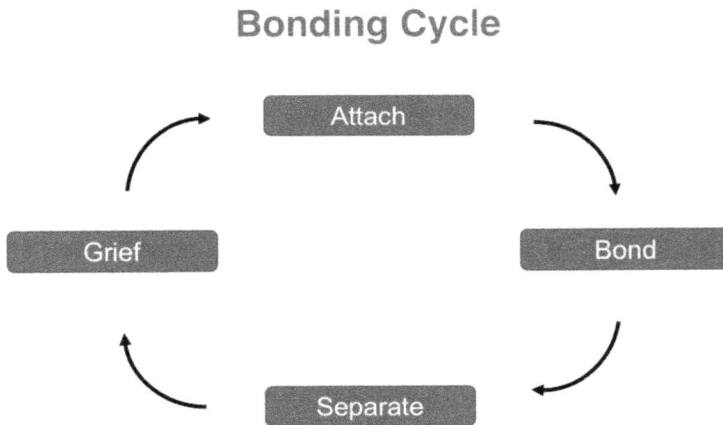

Bonding Cycle

Attach

Bond

Separate

Grief

By George Kohlrieser, Susan Goldsworthy and Duncan Coombe

The first stage of the bonding cycle is an **attachment**. Whether to a new partner, a new job or a new project, people are comfortable when they are attached to someone or something. Everyone needs attachment. It provides a sense of **comfort**. When we feel attached, we feel safe enough to let our natural guards down.

Experiencing attachment means more time is available to work — instead of spending time and energy, and worrying about potential threats.

Bonding is the next stage in the cycle. Not every attachment leads to an emotional bond. Bonding flows from what you do with the connection initiated through attachment. When the attachment leads to a source or exchange of energy, emotion, and depth of contact, the chemistry between people and synergy around a common goal, it transforms into a bond.

A bond is also not limited to people. You can also bond with a purpose, a goal, a country, an animal, a house, a car, a logo, or anything else.

When it relates to people, the depth and strength of the bond will depend on how much **interest** each person shows in the relationship: how much they each care about the attachment and the common goal. Bond a little, and you will get a little flow of energy. Bond deeply and you will unleash enormous potential.

One of the differences between successful and unsuccessful leaders is how well they bond with their team. However, a common misperception is that bonding equals friendship. Having a common goal is enough; you don't have to go out with colleagues on the weekend.

Separation is the third stage in the cycle. All bonds eventually lead to a transition or end. Separation occurs when people change jobs, when projects get completed, when relationships end or change, when a dream is reached or lost, and when people retire or move. Death is also a form of separation. Everything comes to an end at some stage.

Most of the time, people link separation with a sad or negative experience. However, it can also result in something positive such as getting a promotion (and leaving colleagues behind), getting married (and leaving the single life behind) or gaining a degree (and leaving student life behind). Separation is all about letting go and is a **preparation** for something in the future.

The fourth and final stage in the cycle is **grief**, which is an extension of the separation stage. Grief is the experience of saying goodbye to say hello. Grief usually has a negative connotation, but it can also include positive elements like warm memories about the previous situation.

Grief ideally leads to a new attachment or the renewal of an attachment. It involves the emotional experience resulting from the ending or transition of the bond. Completing the cycle means experiencing and expressing the depth of the grief. Grief allows you to expand your **identity**, embrace your future self, and become ready to form new attachments that can lead to new bonds.

The goals of grief are forgiveness, renewal, and rediscovery of the joy in life, work, or marriage.

It is essential to understand that if you cannot grieve, you will never be able to bond effectively. In fact, for some people, their life strategy is to avoid pain or grief by never bonding. They are not willing to take that risk. For these people, the focus stays on the negative side of bonding: the fact that at some stage, it has to end. That's why some people can't commit to a team or a goal.

For every change, however small it is, the stages of *separation* and *grief* need to be passed to connect with the new situation. Whether it's about a new function, team, office, logo, product, software tool, car, computer or suit, people need to go through the separation and grief stage to attach to the new situation. The larger the emotional attachment, the more important it is to go through these stages consciously.

However, in most organizations, little attention is given to grief. Even for events with a major impact like the death of a family or team member, not much time or attention is available for mourning in the western world. No wonder there are so many complaints of employees not being sufficiently engaged. They are stuck in the grief stage and don't have the energy (yet) to attach to the new situation.

Not being able to complete the bonding cycle is one of the reasons why the vibe of people or teams decreases. It's one of the main reasons why change projects fail or don't provide the desired or expected results.

It's also important for leaders to realize that in most cases where change occurs, they're ahead of their team or organization in the bonding cycle. Leaders have typically already gone through some separation and grief and are already attaching themselves to the new situation before they announce it to their team. It's like when a couple breaks up: the person who ends the relationship has already gone through the separation (and even a part of the grieving) stage, while it just starts for their partner. In the enthusiasm to work towards a new goal, leaders often forget that their team needs to go through the separation and grieving stages. This often leads to unnecessary frustration and the misperception of resistance or unwillingness from their teams. This is also one of the reasons why new CEOs or managers with a proven track record are not successful, despite their experience. They didn't allow their team to process grief in their own way — saying goodbye to the former manager, the old way of working or the old team.

A variant of grief is *anticipated grief*. When people assume or fear that they will have to give up something that is important to them in the future, they already go into grief mode. When that is combined with insecurity, people can end up in a negative vibe and stay there for a long time (for they are in grief mode and have no supportive impulses to transition to a new attach phase).

For example, when a global company announces 2,000 employees will be fired over the coming year, a lot of employees will be in grief mode for the next 12 months and usually even longer. This has a huge impact on the vibes of individuals and teams and consequently on the performance of a company. Not only are there less workers, but the remaining employees will be mentally less available as well. This is a huge hidden cost.

The overlooked stage of grief calls for a compassionate attitude, which includes being open to the emotions that come up in this stage and make time and space for them to surface. This usually means slowing down and taking time. However, this is not allowed in most western work environments. The show must go on. What is overlooked though, is that by investing in the grieving stage, time is saved later on when attaching and bonding to the new situation. However, this is not the traditional way of leading or managing a team, mainly because most managers haven't learned how to deal with emotions like sadness and anger.

That's why there is a need for Compassionate Leaders: leaders who feel safe enough to deal with any emotion that comes up. This usually means that they've gone through personal development where they faced their shadow sides, pains, and hurts. It's necessary to have a feeling of inner safety to handle whatever may arise. It's also important to know from personal experience what other people are going through.

When leaders have become Compassionate Leaders, they have laid the foundation for loyal and engaged team members.

There are two important ways to keep team members loyal and engaged. Treat them well in difficult circumstances and support them in becoming a better version of themselves.

Raising these feelings as a leader means being a secure base and, from a compassionate attitude, support co-workers go through the bonding cycle.

Not only will team members become loyal (which means lower costs) and engaged (which means better results), but they will also become raving fans and ambassadors (which means growth).

Compassionate Leaders

Now let's tie what we know about compassion and Compassionate Leadership together with more characteristics to make the picture clear.

In general, a Compassionate Leader is someone who knows what compassion is — and is not — and lives accordingly. A Compassionate Leader acts as a secure base for the team, considers tension a pointer to opportunities for growth, and focuses on increasing their level of Compassionate Leadership. They can take individuals, teams, and organizations to a higher vibe, meaning a higher level of performance and well-being, in a safe and stimulating way when tensions occur.

A Compassionate Leader is also someone who is open-minded and can balance masculine and feminine energy inside themselves, *doing* and *being*, technology/results and humaneness/connections, down-to-earthiness and spirituality, fun and getting stuff done.

A Compassionate Leader is curious about differences and offers a safe space for them to exist. They look for clarity and the essence and root of the matter. They are also vulnerable, which can be a source of strength.

They listen with compassion and speak from the heart. This doesn't mean they communicate in a soft or fluffy way. They can be very direct at addressing pain or tension and pointing people towards their responsibilities. The difference is that they do this with compassion.

A Compassionate Leader is someone who first raises the center of gravity of the vibe of an individual or team and only then announces change. They understand the bonding cycle and can quickly raise the vibe if an event makes it go down.

They are not only more successful and loved by their team, but Compassionate Leaders experience a great deal of freedom. This means that they are not dependent on approval from anyone. They are free from the opinions and judgments of people. They are free from patterns that hold them back. They are free from fears.

Even though a Compassionate Leader can still experience those elements, they are not held hostage by them. Those elements don't shake up their world. Compassionate Leaders can remain present in stressful situations. They can deal with people in victim mode and with uncertainty. By doing this in a compassionate way, they can provide solutions for themselves and their organization. They are able to offer options which nobody thought of before.

By being who they are and by living compassionately, they invite others – unconsciously – to become Compassionate Leaders as well. They inspire by being.

Leading by example can also encompass making mistakes, admitting them, choosing something else and talking about their process. In other words, in my opinion a Compassionate Leader is also someone who hasn't ticked all the boxes yet, but has the heart-felt desire to follow this path and become a genuine Compassionate Leader.

It might feel like a utopian dream to become a Compassionate Leader or see somebody else becoming one. However, it's not difficult once you've made the decision. The steps to becoming a Compassionate Leader by following the Compassionate Leader Pathway are described in chapter 11.

Benefits of Compassionate Leaders

Besides experiencing more freedom, let's look at other benefits of being a Compassionate Leader.

Personal benefits

In their book, *An Everyone Culture: Becoming a Deliberately Developmental Organization,* authors Robert Kegan and Lisa Laskow Lahey write: "Someone once said that we admire people because of the strength they display, but that we feel personally attracted to them because of the vulnerability they show us."

Compassionate Leaders can show both strength and vulnerability. That's one of the reasons why Compassionate Leaders can attract and keep top talent, even if another company offers more money or extra benefits.

On a professional level, Compassionate Leaders:
- receive the most interesting projects;
- have better performing teams;
- reach their goals easily;
- enjoy harmony within their team.

On a personal level, Compassionate Leaders:
- are more relaxed;
- have less stress;
- have greater problem-solving abilities;
- are more in touch with all aspects of life;
- receive more love and compassion;
- are more fulfilled.

In other words, they are happier and more successful in both their personal and professional lives.

Benefits for the organization

Besides providing inspirational examples for co-workers, companies with Compassionate Leaders experience the following benefits (according to Monica Worline and Jane Dutton in their book *Awakening Compassion At Work)*.

Compassion motivates **innovation by inspiring** new ideas and creating psychological safety that enhances learning. When leaders are compassionate, they offer a safe space to share crazy ideas on the one hand and failures or fears on the other. This leads to more open discussions about errors and potential solutions. People are not punished when they offer different opinions or show their vulnerability. On the contrary, curiosity is encouraged.

Compassion infuses rapid **coordination and collaboration** with respect, trust and strong human connections. This increases people's willingness and ability to work together for mutual benefit. Especially in today's complex multinational organizations with matrix structures, there is a need for another way to collaborate than in command and control environments. Compassion is a key element to get the job done with people that don't have any reward or punishment capacities towards each other.

Compassion in **recruiting** helps to find and keep the right people by increasing commitment and cultural fit. Experiencing compassion (giving it, receiving it and even witnessing it) as part of the work environment builds commitment, which helps organizations keep talented people. In the same respect, compassion increases **employee engagement**. And according to Gallup's research, engaged employees create engaged customers and those engaged customers spend more money, more often with their preferred brands.

Compassion fuels **adaptability**. Adaptability to change is at the heart of sustaining strategic competitive advantage over time. It has become a truism that change is a constant in organizational life. However, the difficulty and pain associated with change often goes unaddressed. Many times, the driver for change is a new technology. A lot of IT projects don't get finished as planned or don't deliver the expected results. An important factor is that the human tensions inside and between people are often ignored. Acknowledging these tensions and dealing with them in a compassionate way makes a huge difference. Research has shown that people who are affected by change done with compassion are less likely to resist and more likely to invest in making change effective. The reason is that not only the bonding cycle is taken into account, but also managed in a compassionate way while using the right techniques.

Societal benefits

Since individuals and organizations can no longer exist independently in this super-connected world, there are instant ripple effects.

Compassionate Leaders who inspire their organizations, transfer this compassion to the whole ecosystem: customers, suppliers, partners, media, families of employees, local communities, and all other stakeholders.

In other words: everyone benefits!

Key Take-Aways

When it's about compassion, there are two key insights. There is a distinction between suffering and pain. The translation of the word *compassion* is *be with pain suffering* not *suffer with*.

Compassion is being able to be with someone without suffering yourself — even if they're having a hard time or behaving negatively. It's about seeing them as a fellow, equivalent human being, not as a victim. It's about being able to keep a focus on their talents and positive qualities, while allowing the pain to be expressed, no matter how small or large. That way, the other person can be supported in a safe and stimulating way.

The bonding cycle is a dynamic which is usually overlooked when any sort of change happens or when change projects are executed.

These are the four stages:

- Attachment, which provides some comfort;
- Bonding, which is defined by the level of interest experienced in the relationship;
- Separation, which prepares us for any new situation beyond grief;
- Grieving, which can expand your identity and embrace your future self.

The level of Compassionate Leadership is a major contributor to the bonding cycle that a team can go through. The definition of Compassionate Leadership is: "The ability to take individuals, teams, and organizations to a higher vibe, meaning a higher level of performance and well-being, in a safe and stimulating way when tensions occur."

Compassionate Leaders are people who have chosen to apply compassion in the workplace.

They act as *secure bases* for the team and value differences. They are balanced (masculine/feminine, doing/being, down-to-earth/spirituality) and consider tension as a pointer to growth. They are always looking for clarity and the essence of a situation beyond the surface. They can raise the vibe of their team, especially when a setback occurs.

Professionally, Compassionate Leaders attract the most interesting projects, have the highest performing teams, and can attract and keep top talent — even when they can't pay as much as other organizations. They are able to create the space for an inspiring vibe.

Personally, Compassionate Leaders are more relaxed, experience less stress, have higher problem-solving qualities, and experience more love and compassion. They also experience more emotional freedom.

The benefits for an organization are:

- Compassion motivates innovation through new ideas while creating psychological safety to enhance learning.
- Compassion infuses rapid coordination and collaboration with respect, trust, and strong human connections. It increases a willingness and the ability to work together for mutual benefit.
- Compassion in recruiting helps find and keep the right people by increasing commitment and creating the right cultural fit.

- Compassion increases employee engagement. According to Gallup's research, engaged employees create engaged customers, and engaged customers spend more money, more often with their preferred brands.
- Compassion fuels adaptability by alleviating the pain caused by change and sparking a passion that motivates resourceful change.

Since individuals and organizations can no longer exist independently in this super-connected world, there are instant ripple effects for stakeholders, the ecosystem of the organization and society as a whole.

Chapter 4

Blocks to Raising the Vibe

As you learned from the previous chapters, raising the vibe is increasingly important when dealing with current and future challenges.

It is the combination of external and internal factors that define whether or not the vibe is raised. Practical or process tensions, interpersonal tensions and personal tensions show where there are opportunities to raise the vibe.

In this chapter, we will look at the underlying dynamics of personal tension. Personal tensions are strongly related to personal development and the growth of consciousness. They are also the most important blocks towards the rise of the vibe.

One of the most powerful dynamics on a personal level is called the ego. So, let's start with looking at what it's about and which strategies it uses. We can then explore how to use them as a pointer when blocks hinder the development of our consciousness. The last step is to see how those blocks can be transformed. As a result, space is created to rise to an inspiring vibe.

The Leader and the Ego

"He has a big ego" is a common phrase when talking about leaders. But what does that mean?

In the Oxford Dictionary, the definition of ego is "a person's sense of self-esteem or self-importance."

If we put this in the phrase, "He has a big ego," it becomes, "He has a great sense of self-esteem or self-worth."

Now this feels weird, doesn't it? It feels more like the opposite: "He has a big *need to defend or increase* his sense of self-esteem or self-worth."

This means that he doesn't feel safe (yet) to show himself as he is with both his qualities and shadow sides.

Let's read that sentence again: "He has a big *need to defend or increase* his sense of self-esteem or self-worth." Don't you feel that just reading that sentence changes the energy? When I look at it this way, I can be much more compassionate towards this person and his behavior.

So, the ego is the mechanism that acts to defend or increase the sense of self-esteem or self-worth. To be able to use the entry point of the ego to raise the vibe, it's important to get a deeper understanding of how it works. So, let's look at five strategies that are linked to the ego.

Strategy 1: Judging

Judging is the result of identifying with certain thoughts and valuing them.

Because it's important to understand what's going on, let's look at what I call the *experience model*.

1. All-day long, we think thoughts and hear other people's opinions.
2. Some thoughts and opinions we value as true and others as false. As a consequence, behavior in line with what is true, is right and desirable, while unaligned behavior is wrong and despicable.
3. The longer we give attention to a thought, the more it becomes a belief. The more important we deem a belief, and the more we identify with it, the more intense our experiences around that thought will be.
4. The more the thoughts and beliefs that we have valued as true are confirmed, the more relaxed we are (the ego is at rest). The more those true thoughts or beliefs are denied, or, the more the thought that we have valued as false is triggered, the more stressed we are (the ego is active, it is looking for ways to attack/defend).
5. We react, verbally or physically (fight or flight) or we don't react and keep it to ourselves (freeze).

Step 2 is where judgment originates. The moment we label something as right or wrong, we have judged something. The height and severity of our judgment are created in steps 3 and 4.

> An example of judging is when Ariane blamed her colleague Christine in the customer service department for being too vague (see chapter 1).

The danger of judging is that it keeps people stuck in the bonding cycle, specifically in the bond phase of the old situation. Judging holds us in the old situation and blocks us from the new situation (the separate and grief phases).

Strategy 2: Projection

Before we look at projection, let's have another look at judging.

When we label something as true or false, we automatically start to judge. What is true becomes right and what is false (or the opposite of what is deemed right) becomes wrong. The stronger our feelings are about that thought, the stronger we're likely to express our judgment with shouting, strong adjectives, superlatives, accusations and exaggerations (using words like always or never).

When judgment is about someone's character or personality, our reaction usually looks like this:

- "She is *amazingly* well mannered. She *always* wishes me a good morning."
- "He is *incredibly* dependent on others. He can *never* do something on his own."
- "She has *such* good taste. She *always* wears nice clothes."
- "She is *awfully* critical. She *always* has a comment or opinion to voice about everything. Nothing is *ever* good enough for her."
- "He is so *deeply* respectful. He *always* opens the door for his wife and treats her like a real lady."
- "He is *utterly* lazy. He *never* finishes his work on time."

So why does the ego value some thoughts as wanted behavior or acceptable opinions, but also judges other thoughts as unwanted behavior or unacceptable opinions?

The ego judges thoughts good or bad, wanted, or undesirable because it relates those thoughts to how to deal with a situation. When the ego notices something that is in line with what it perceives to be true, it deems the situation safe, at least for now. When it notices something that seems false or opposite to what is true, an alert about a possible attack is triggered. The ego knows that it should start to defend itself or attack the potential perpetrator as a precaution.

One way to defend itself is to **project** the thoughts, fears and what is valued as wrong onto the situation or person.

How does projection work?

Projection is always about something inside ourselves that we don't like.

However, instead of looking at it, we separate ourselves from it by dissociating from it. Then we throw it (or project it) onto someone else.

Because it is now separated from us and associated with someone else, it is not our problem anymore (at least, that is the strategy of projection). Moreover, the ego can now defend itself against it so it won't come back to haunt or disturb it.

When we dissociate the experience, we don't have a relationship with it anymore. As a consequence, our projection can be attacked; it can be seen as worthless; it can be disposed of and, best of all, it can be seen as someone else's issue or problem, allowing us to escape the pain of owning it in ourselves.

> An example of projection is how account manager Jeffrey projected *his* aversion for homework on the marketing team in chapter 2. He blamed them for not doing *their* homework.

> Another example are gay politicians and religious leaders who have a hard time with their nature and who have unleashed witch hunts on gay people.

Strategy 3: Victimhood

When we feel disrespected, disadvantaged, or attacked in any way, most of us fall into some kind of **victim** role. Sometimes this can feel very heavy, at other times rather moderate. Sometimes we are aware of it, and sometimes we aren't. But the message we tell ourselves (unconsciously) is: "Poor me, it's not fair."

Complaining about it is one of the most common ways to deal with this feeling of unfairness. It is about justifying our victimhood.

Most of us step into the victim role easily enough, but we do so even quicker if it looks like the attacker or the threat seems too big or too overwhelming to react to without being physically or mentally hurt.

In other cases, we take a different approach. When the attacker is not aware that we perceive the threat, we are more likely to be the first to attack. We attack because it seems to be the best defense, especially when we can add an element of surprise. Then something really interesting happens. To get out of the victim role (defending ourselves), we step into the **persecutor or perpetrator** role (attacking others).

By attacking the other person, we take away their (potential) power to attack us. We weaken them. Although it seems that launching an initial attack will keep us safe, that approach creates a very unstable situation. The person we've just attacked (verbally or physically) may suddenly find some extra ammunition, power or resources somewhere else and come back much stronger. In other words, the ego needs to be vigilant at all times.

> An example of victim behavior can be found in how customer service agent Ariane reacted in chapter 1 to the news that one of the team members probably will get fired and how she responded to her manager Hans when he gave her detailed instructions.

A subtle variation to the persecutor role is becoming the **rescuer**. Although the rescuer-victim relationship is seen as a positive version of the persecutor-victim relationship, it is more or less the same.

The idea behind this victim-rescuer strategy is that we perceive someone as weak, so we become their rescuer. One underlying reason is that we appear so big and strong ourselves that we can't be attacked. Sometimes the unconscious strategy of keeping the other person small, so they don't have enough power to attack us, is at play as well.

> An example of this rescuer behavior was shown in chapter 1 when customer service manager Hans micromanaged team member Ariane by giving her very detailed and unnecessary instructions.

Sometimes you see victimhood turn up in the bonding cycle. When someone is forced to go to the third stage (separation), they might feel like a victim. That's why it's necessary to give enough context and to provide options. Another example is when a person feels like a victim and refuses to let go of a situation. They can't move from the *bonding* to the *separation* phase. In that case, it might help to release the stress first by applying the Compassion Technique or the ABCs of De-stressing (see chapter 7) and then explore what the deeper need or concern is by using Compassionate Communication (see chapter 9).

Strategy 4: Self-criticism

A combination of strategy 1 (judging) and strategy 3 (victimhood) is self-criticism. Often, we are harder on ourselves than we would be on other human beings.

The ego's strategy behind this is that if we attack ourselves first, then we take away the ammunition for other people. The idea behind it is: "I'm already suffering, weak and small, so, there is no reason to attack me."

In her book *Self-Compassion: The Proven Power of Being Kind to Yourself,* author Kristin Neff adds another reason. She writes that in the West the idea has grown that if we are not hard for ourselves we get lazy. We don't get anything accomplished if we are not our own harshest critic.

Another strategy that is linked to self-criticism is comparing ourselves with others. In essence this is good, it is a step towards maturity. Comparing ourselves with others is a natural thing to do. We can see how we are progressing and where we might need to change. We can also see what we need to do to survive.

According to Kristin Neff, this pattern has received an extra impulse by the self-esteem movement. Self-esteem focuses on how we are different from others. In most cases, it means how we are better than others. This causes a separation from other people on the one hand and suffering on the other (especially when combined with strategies of the ego). Why? There will always be someone better.

The way to get out of this pattern is to see our common humanity. This is a different kind of comparing. It's not a case of being better or different from others, but to connect to what we have in common. For example, when we have a bad day, we don't compare ourselves with a colleague who is always in a great mood. We relate to other people who also have a bad day from time to time.

> An example of self-criticism was shown in chapter 1 when account manager James compares himself with his colleagues Saskia and Gary. He compares himself with Saskia regarding the slick layout of her slides and with Gary regarding his light and humorous presentation style. He overlooks the fact that Saskia's presentation style is rather serious and that Gary often forgets to use the latest version of the slides because of his chaotic nature. By only seeing their best qualities

and then adding them, he creates a non-existent superhuman. Every comparison James makes, will be in his disadvantage and will make him feel small and unhappy.

Strategy 5: Unsolicited Advice

Another way of ending up in a stressful situation is giving or receiving unsolicited advice.

I have noticed that in general most people truly want to help others by sharing advice. They share about what worked for them, what they experienced, tips they have received, experts that can be consulted, and books to be read. This is especially true for leaders.

Although the advice is usually shared with good intentions, the reaction of the ones receiving the advice isn't always positive. They often defend themselves or react in a bitter or even hateful way. They might also remain silent and do nothing with the advice offered. They keep suffering, make the same mistakes, and perform below par.

What happens here?

This is another example of the rescuer-victim pattern.

When we share advice without someone asking for it, we violate personal boundaries. The person offering the advice is taking the rescuer role (usually without even being aware of it). As a consequence, the other person is automatically put in the victim role. Although this other person is usually not aware of it either, they feel that something isn't right. They don't want this energy, and their reaction can be fierce. When the reaction is out of proportion, they are probably triggered by old pain as well.

How do you deal with this situation?

If you have given unsolicited advice and the reaction has already happened, the only thing you can do is apologize and back off. It may change the situation. The other person might also apologize, and peace is restored. However, the other person may stay angry. If that's the case, at least you know what the cause was, and you can change your approach the next time.

If you haven't shared any advice yet, the best thing to do is ask for permission or try something like: "I might have a good suggestion, are you interested in hearing it?"

When you do this the other person feels respected. They will also be more open to what you have to say. The reason is that your polite question interrupts their internal speech or thinking pattern.

In some cases, the other person is so deeply immersed in their thought process that they don't even hear you asking the question. However hard it might be, refrain from advising when that happens.

Sometimes it is the other way around: someone is offering unsolicited advice to you. They step into the rescuer role, and you feel the victim energy.

When that occurs, notice what happened before. Often, you were complaining or venting.

When people complain or vent, they usually aren't looking for a solution. They simply need to get rid of annoying energy. They – unconsciously – need to get rid of tension. This is not nice energy to be around for someone else. This other person doesn't want this energy and uses – also unconsciously – a strategy to eliminate this energy. One of the most used strategies is offering unsolicited advice.

These processes that happen on a deeper level give rise to tension between people on the surface. So, when you feel like a victim because the other person shared unsolicited advice with you, look at your part in the process. Were you complaining or venting?

As a summary, these are my suggestions when you feel the urge to share advice: be respectful, ask for permission, and let go if someone is not ready to hear what you have to say. It will help you avoid new tensions and improve the relationship.

> An example of unsolicited advice is how customer service manager Hans told his team member Ariane how to do her work (see chapter 1).

Inner Parts

After having explored five of the most common strategies of the ego, it's time to dig a bit deeper.

When someone says, "You have a big ego" or "Leave your ego at the door," you may feel a kind of resistance. When you voice this resistance, people may say that your ego is defending itself. At least, this has been my experience.

When it happened, I felt that it was partially true. Yes, there was a part of me that made itself bigger or more important to get more attention or to defend itself. However, there was also the feeling that it was just a part of me. It's not all of me, and it doesn't define who I am.

After years of research and self-inquiry, I have discovered that those exact words are the key to transformation: "This is not all of me; this doesn't define who I am." It's the parts inside me that show a certain behavior for known or unknown reasons.

We all have several parts inside ourselves that work together or have opposite longings or needs. For example:

> When the alarm clock goes off in the morning, a part of us wants to stay in bed, and another part wants to get up or feels obliged to get up.

> When a friend invites you to a movie, a part of you wants to go, and another part wants to stay home.

> Most people have a part that is very dutiful and another part that is a party animal. In some people, duty seems to be lacking. In other people, it's the party animal. However, when circumstances change, the other part can be instantly present. The 100 percent party animal might become dutiful in a crisis. For people who seem to be 100 percent dutiful, the party animal might come out after a few alcoholic drinks.

Usually, we can quickly decide which part to follow, but sometimes it's a real struggle. And even if we make a quick decision, sometimes a nagging feeling or voice is saying, "Shouldn't I have done the opposite?"

This gives way to tension in ourselves. This gives way to a kind of *personal* tension. And just like you read in chapter 2, this tension usually seeks a way out in the interaction with other people, which leads to *interpersonal* tension.

This is not a nice feeling and not what we want. However, the good news is that if we follow the opposite route, we can get to the core of what is happening and balance the two inner parts. In other words, we can use interpersonal tension as a pointer to what needs to be balanced in ourselves. Instead of being angry at other people, we can be grateful for the pointers they offer us.

Before we do that, let's take a deeper look into the dynamics of inner parts to understand what needs to be balanced.

Primary selves versus disowned selves

Hal and Sidra Stone call these inner parts our selves. Hal and Sidra paved the way with *Voice Dialogue*, a method that brings those different parts in ourselves to the forefront. It provides clarity in their behavior, needs, and longings.

One of the important findings of their research was that we have *primary selves* and *disowned selves*.

A *primary self* is a part of us that is very present. It's also pretty dominant and demanding.

A *disowned self* is a part of us that has no or very little room.

When we go back to the example of dutiful versus party animal, in some people the dutiful part is a primary self, and the party animal is a disowned self. In other people, it's the other way around.

Where does the behavior of each part come from? Although every case is different, it usually comes from experiences in childhood or impactful events.

In childhood, we needed to develop certain strategies or adapt to other people to survive.

For example:

> Bart was praised for his good grades at school and got an extra allowance because of them. This led to a primary self that became very focused on rational activities and performing. His emotional self became disowned.

Whenever he made any noise as a young child, Danny was punished by his dad. This led to the development of a primary self that is quiet and introvert. His joyful and extraverted self became disowned.

When Eric was little, there wasn't much food for the family. It was sometimes a fight between siblings to get potatoes at dinner time. As the smallest child, Eric often got the least amount of food and was hungry all the time. This led to a primary self that takes care of itself first, even at the expense of other people. The self that takes other people's interests into account became disowned.

So, what happens is that an imbalance is created between two inner parts. In Bart's case, the rational self became dominant, and the emotional self is put away in a corner. This encourages the behavior of the primary self. Meanwhile, the behavior of the disowned self is discouraged. In other words, we look at the world through specific glasses now. It becomes a self-fulfilling prophecy.

For example, when Bart gets good grades again, his family congratulates him. When he cries, he is ignored or mocked. In the first case, his primary self is strengthened. In the second case, his disowned self is weakened.

A self is always linked to a core quality, with something positive. However, when that quality needs to be protected, the *behavior* of the self can be negative. It becomes a negative excess of a positive quality.

In Bart's case, for example, the protective behavior of his rational self can be acting coldly and rigidly without taking other people's feelings into account. This behavior is not always present but shows up if he feels that his rational side might come under pressure or when people are showing too much of their emotional side.

This happens every time his rational side gets triggered. As a result, a pattern is created at an unconscious level. Those patterns can become so strong that even in a crisis (his wife leaving him), the pattern continues.

The good news is that those patterns (or mental models) are only created based on experiences. They are not genetic or set in stone. In other words, they can be changed.

By looking at them with gratitude and compassion, and by noticing that they are pointers towards the root instead of something that needs to be cut out (or numbed), something fundamental can be transformed.

Instead of trying to banish the problem (the excessive behavior of the primary self), we might see it as an important part of the solution.

The first reason that I'm sharing this is that these insights will make you more compassionate towards your own irrational behavior and that of others. More compassion means more room for solutions.

The second reason is that it will allow you to notice behavior that is a consequence of this mechanism. Then you can deal with it with more awareness and choose to behave differently.

The third reason is that now you know how this works, you will probably be more open to tools and techniques to solve the blocks so you and your team can grow. One of the techniques is the Inner Balance Technique (see chapter 8) that allows you to bring back an equilibrium between a primary and disowned self. Once they are balanced, they reinforce rather than fight each other. Not only will you feel more inner harmony, but you can reach your goals faster and with less effort.

Once we are aware that only a small part of ourselves is being criticized or is behaving in an unhealthy way, we can be more compassionate and better support ourselves. This realization can help us to stay out of a defensive reaction and out of a victim mode. It can also help us to be more open for self-discovery: we are now more able to look at the inner part that needs attention or is damaging social contact, teamwork or results. We can now start to understand it better and look for ways to balance it.

The Ego Revisited

Let's get back to the ego and its strategies. Another perspective on those strategies is that they are used to protect us. And just as important, we now know it is a primary or disowned self that is applying them.

As a result, I consider the *ego* the umbrella term for all the inner selves, with both their qualities and negative behavior. It is the negative behavior we usually have in mind when we use the term *ego*. As long as we keep using this umbrella term, together with the focus on negative behavior, nothing can get solved. When you focus on negative behavior, it puts the people involved in an attacker-defender position, where no attention can be given to the underlying qualities.

To change our perspective, let's look back at the five strategies and translate them with this new perspective of inner parts.

> When customer service employee Ariane is judging Christine for being too vague (which could be an excess of the core quality of being flexible), something in Ariane is trying to protect her. There is a part of her that is trying to protect her core quality of clarity. By being heavily focused on clarity, she has become rigid (excess of clarity) and could use more flexibility to balance it out.

> When account manager Jeffrey is projecting his aversion for homework on the marketing department, something is trying to protect him. There is a part in him that is trying to shield him from being criticized because of below-par homework/input.

> When Ariane is feeling like a victim when her manager Hans tries to help her, a part of her is trying to protect her. By yelling, she is trying to scare her perceived attacker away and keep him at a distance in the future. But this doesn't leave any space for the part of her that could use some (respectful) support from others.

> When Hans is trying to rescue Ariane, he is also trying to protect himself. When focusing on someone else, there is no need or room for self-inquiry. This puts the parts that protect Hans at ease. Also, when Hans is offering unsolicited advice, a part of him is seeking protection. By sharing advice, the focus is put on his parts that are deemed positive and helpful (primary selves), and the attention is diverted from his disowned selves.

> When account manager James is criticizing himself for not being a good presenter, something inside is looking for protection. By sharing the argument that he is not performing well, a part of him is already preparing for the attack from others and giving them less ammunition. While this might have worked in the past, balancing it with his positive qualities will help him grow.

Once we know that someone's negative ego behavior is actually about inner parts, the situation changes. Once we know it is just a part that tries to protect them, we can be more compassionate towards their behavior.

In his book, *Nonviolent Communication: A Language of Life*, the words of author Marshall Rosenberg help me whenever people start judging or blaming others. "Every judgment is an unmet need."

I would like to add "… from an inner part."

When we can look through these glasses, we can start to explore why this is happening or what is needed to satisfy the other person's needs without triggering those protective strategies and behavior.

The same applies to us. Once we understand that one inner part of us can protect us from unwanted behavior from another inner part, we can be more compassionate and less critical.

Instead of saying "I should be more relaxed," you can say "Hmm, it seems that there is a part in me that wants to work all the time, which doesn't leave much space for the part in me that wants to relax."

Just reframing the situation makes a huge difference. You could do the same when observing others. Instead of saying to Kent: "You should not want to be in the spotlight the whole time," you can say "Hmm, apparently there is a part in Kent that needs a lot of attention, which doesn't leave much space for the part in him that uses other people's input to improve his ideas." First you can do this in silence. This will help to be more compassionate towards him and approach him differently. The next step could be to share it with him verbally.

Authenticity

There is a lot of talk about being authentic as a leader.

Every time I hear that leaders have to be more authentic, I wonder if the speaker understands what they are saying.

My perception is that they have a longing for leaders to show their humane side, where they care for others and not treat them as a number in a spreadsheet.

For me, this is a first step. It is a step that can support many teams transition from a negative into a neutral vibe or from a neutral into a positive vibe. However, it is just the first step.

To me, being authentic means facing all inner parts. It means facing the ones you deem positive and the ones you deem negative. It is about both the primary and the disowned selves.

Being able and willing to face them is one part. Being able and willing to talk about the fears and shames that pop up during the discovery process is an important second part.

That's not easy, but the rewards are high. Life becomes easier, less complex, more fulfilling, and more joyful. You transition into the inspiring vibe and open the gateway for your team or organization to do the same.

Discovering Inner Parts

Since the pattern of primary and disowned selves is an unconscious one, it's not always immediately clear which inner parts are at play. Before they can be balanced, we need to know which selves are involved. There are two simple ways to detect them: listening to your own inner voices and using inter-personal tension as a pointer.

Listening to your inner voices

The first way to detect inner parts is to listen to inner voices. Listen to your self-talk: notice a strong opinion or criticism in your behavior. Usually, these are your primary selves talking.

Disowned selves are harder to hear since they have been put in the proverbial corner. However, sometimes, you hear them. They can also have some criticism, or they can feel sad.

The key to balancing oneself is to make a distinction between their qualities and excesses and to be grateful for the role the primary selves played.

For example, let's suppose Paul has an inner self that wants to go to a party and another inner self that wants to stay home. We could call the first inner self an extravert and the second inner self an introvert.

This is how the inner dialogue could go:
- Extravert: "Let's go to this party!"
- Introvert: "No, let's stay home."

- Extravert: "Don't be such an asocial hermit. If you don't go out, you won't make any friends, and nobody will like you anymore."
- Introvert: "I don't want to go. I need some rest. We already went to two parties this week. I need to recharge my batteries. Besides, these parties are full of superficial conversations and drunk people."

Depending on which inner self is the strongest, Paul goes to the party or stays home. But what happens a lot is that the other self is nagging in the background or having regrets. If Paul is at the party, the introvert voice might be pointing out all the drunks and regrets that Paul didn't stay at home. If Paul stays at home, the extravert might be saying that Paul will stay single forever.

What happens here is that the inner selves are criticizing certain aspects of each other, the excesses. And they overlook each other's qualities.

In the example of Paul going to a party versus staying home, it looks like this:
- Going to a party:
  o Excesses: superficial conversations, drunk people and energy drain;
  o Qualities: connecting with other people, dancing and new friends.
- Staying at home:
  o Excesses: asocial, hermit and selfish;
  o Qualities: recharge batteries, resting and gaining knowledge by reading a book.

The first clue to balancing these inner selves is to focus on the qualities of each self instead of the potential excesses.

The second clue is to be grateful for the work of the primary self. The primary self became a primary self out of concern and protection. An inner self becomes a primary self to survive. This is a vital role.

The role is primarily crucial in childhood. Later on in life, we see that there are more options, and we can take care of ourselves in several ways. However, by then, the behavior of the primary self has already become an automatic, unconscious pattern. This makes it more difficult to detect our inner parts. That's why the second way of detecting primary and disowned selves is usually an easier approach (see the section "Using interpersonal tension as a pointer" below).

At the same moment we are grateful for the role the primary self has played, we can have compassion for the disowned self. That inner part was put in the background so it wouldn't stand in the way of the survival mechanism. In most people, this disowned self has agreed to go along and sit in the corner.

In some people, the disowned self didn't comply, and their struggle is often obvious to the outside world. Depending on the situation, the disowned self can show itself occasionally or very often. If it is disowned and is not allowed to be present, it usually shows itself in extreme behavior. For example, the party animal that is not allowed to be present according to the dutiful self, can get very drunk at a birthday party of a family member. This is a good example of how it's not about having fun (quality) anymore, but about showing excessive behavior as a cry for attention.

When a pair of primary and disowned selves are balanced, the result is that:
- The primary self can get some rest. It doesn't have to be so vigilant anymore or take care of everything.
- The disowned self can be present more and add its qualities to the mix, which leads to a more fulfilling and richer life.

Using interpersonal tension as a pointer

The second way to detect your primary and disowned selves is to pay attention when you feel interpersonal tension. This tension is usually obvious with people you spend more time with like colleagues or a life partner.

The first step is to pay attention to whom is being criticized for what.

When people are giving *comments on your behavior*, it's usually about the excesses of one of your *primary* selves.

When *you criticize other people*, it's usually about excesses of behavior that is linked to your *disowned* selves.

The next step is to define the underlying qualities of the detected self.

A great tool to help you with these steps is called Compassion Quadrants. You will find it in chapter 8.

Finding the inner selves is not so difficult to do, but not many people succeed because they get stuck in the battle of criticizing the excesses. This pushes people in an offensive or defensive position. In a defensive position, the focus is on the (potential) attacker, not on the underlying qualities. In an offensive position, the focus is on the excesses, not on the underlying qualities either.

That's why we need a compassionate attitude. When we can go into compassion mode instead of a defensive stance, we can start looking for the selves that are not in balance. Then we can explore their qualities. This can bring some peace to the situation. Then the Inner Balance Technique can be used (see chapter 8) to balance the inner selves. The result is that they will start reinforcing each other.

Key Take-Aways

When people talk about someone having a big ego, they usually judge this person as being arrogant. In most cases, it boils down to someone who feels the need to protect themselves.

Five of the most commonly used protection strategies are judging, projecting, victimhood, self-criticism, and unsolicited advice.

However, most people are not aware that they apply one of those strategies, nor that some kind of protection mechanism is behind it.

It is an inner self that is taking control. This is usually a primary self.

The primary self is defending us from reliving pain from the past or is applying a pattern that helped us to adapt. It helped us survive as a child or during an impactful moment.

The consequence is that another complementary part is disowned. This disowned self also asks for attention from time to time. It depends on the power of the primary self whether or not it succeeds. Both the asking for attention by a disowned self and the repression by a primary self are usually expressed as negative or excessive behavior.

As long as we don't look into this imbalance in ourselves, it will play out in our lives. Other people will trigger us by showing the same excessive behavior as our disowned selves.

This doesn't always feel good since the excessive behavior of the primary selves of the two people involved can lead to a fight. On the other hand, it is great that this happens. It provides us with an entry point to disowned selves that otherwise would remain in a blind spot.

The more compassionate we can be, the easier it becomes to detect when those dynamics are at play. It also becomes easier to both end the fight and learn something about ourselves. However, that is not always easy in the heat of the moment. That's why it's important to have leaders or other facilitators with a high level of Compassionate Leadership available until everybody is capable of being compassionate enough when there are arguments.

When we can balance the primary and disowned selves, we can develop further as a person and raise our vibe. Our lives become easier as well since there is no energy spent suppressing the disowned self. Moreover, the two selves are now reinforcing each other.

An excellent tool to detect the primary and disowned selves are Compassion Quadrants. Then those selves can be integrated using the Inner Balance Technique. You will find these tools in chapter 8.

Chapter 5

Transforming Tension:

the D.U.E.T. process

When tensions are transformed, the vibe rises. This makes it easier and more enjoyable to work together, and performance increases. One ingredient of success is that this process is facilitated by someone whose level of Compassionate Leadership is high enough.

A second ingredient involves techniques to transform the tensions. In this chapter, we will look into how to do this using the D.U.E.T. process. It includes several tools and techniques. Which tools and techniques are used depends on the kind of tension that is experienced: practical/process, personal or interpersonal tension.

It is also important to transform tensions and consequently raise the vibe as preparation for change projects. When team members are in a positive or inspiring vibe, they tend to focus on the opportunities that change brings instead of resisting it. When they have the techniques of the D.U.E.T. process at their disposal, they will be able to deal with the unavoidable tensions that come with any change project. This allows them to quickly bounce back instead of getting stuck in a negative vibe.

You will find an overview of the steps and techniques in this chapter. The detailed instructions on how to apply each technique can be found in the next chapters.

Navigating via Tension

If we want our teams and organizations to thrive, we need to face tension instead of ignoring it. Tension can feel positive (excitement) or negative (fear).

In its the essence, tension is a neutral signal that something wants to change or wants to grow. That's why the phrase "navigating via tension" is used in methodologies like Holacracy and Sociocracy 3.0 (S3).

It is not always easy to look at tension or to support an individual or a team face one. That's why there is a focus on Compassionate Leadership in this book. It makes it so much easier to face the tensions that come up.

When the word *compassion* is used, most people tend to focus on the negative tensions. But it also applies to the positive ones.

Why? Because we are not used to dealing with any kind of tension. Most of the time, we push tensions away, ignore them, or project them to someone or something else. In all those cases, we don't have to feel them.

For example, when account manager Jeffrey feels tension about not acquiring enough customers, these are the usual coping strategies:
- Ignore the tension and just keep doing the same thing.
- Push the tension away and hope that a change will occur spontaneously.
- Project it on something (bad economy) or someone (marketing is doing a bad job) and keep complaining about those external circumstances.

The reason that human beings use one of these strategies is that it seems easier to deal with the situation we know (how uncomfortable it may be) than with unknown circumstances — the new situation tension invites us to look at.

This is the case for both a situation where some kind of suffering, pain, or a (potential) threat is present and a situation where a growth opportunity presents itself. A compassionate approach is needed in both cases to understand the tension and transform it. By the way, one of the lesser-known reasons for burnout is not being incapable of coping with the workload; it's not being able to understand (and act upon) tension. In other words, it's about a lack of clarity of the situation.

Clarity

Bringing clarity is not only a characteristic of a Compassionate Leader. It is easier, in general, to be compassionate if we understand what is going on. That's why the main goal of this book is providing clarity and insight.

When I talk about clarity, there is a metaphor I like to use: life can be like a ball of yarn.

Individual events and their related tensions can be so intertwined that it's not clear where one tension ends and another starts.

When you want to make a dark-colored scarf, you can use the threads with the darkest colors. You don't need the other ones. When you look at this pile of yarn, it's not clear which dark-colored threads are entangled with the other threads. However, you can't do anything with the pile as a whole. You need to pick one thread. Even though there are other threads, you need to stay focused on the darkest-colored one.

The same applies to deal with tension.

It's important to focus on one tension at a time. If more tensions show up, name them, and put them aside for the time being. For example, you can put them on a list to deal with later.

> Let's go back to Gizmo Objects Inc. and take the example of customer service agent Frank, who complains that the communication in the company is bad. His new manager Catherine hears his complaint.
>
> Catherine has replaced Hans, who is at home and burned out. The negative vibe of the team finally got to him. He wonders what happened. He had always been a positive person, but no matter what he tried with the team, there was always resistance. Even when team members promised to do a certain task, they would stop the moment his back was turned. Much to his frustration, the successful approach he had used with other teams in the past hadn't worked at all. The result was burnout.

When Catherine had been asked to lead the customer service department until Hans returned, she had needed some time to think about it. That department was known for its flare-ups and toxic atmosphere. When she had inquired why she had been asked to take over, CEO John and COO Helen had told her that they had been impressed by the way she had handled several change projects in the past and how she had dealt with the related tensions. Those were skills that could come in handy when leading the customer service department. The trust that John and Helen had in her had been the decisive factor in Catherine accepting the new role. Catherine had felt that John and Helen were secure bases for her. However, she knew she had to be careful. The previous team she had managed was in a positive vibe. She knew she had to be careful not to automatically use the same approach to a team with a negative vibe. Otherwise, she might end up like Hans.

When Catherine hears Frank's complaint about bad communication, she notices that it is such an abstract sentence that she can't do anything with it. Although Catherine intends to support Frank and do something about the situation, it is not clear for her yet where to start. She already has an idea of what can be done, but chances are her solution won't be the one that helps Frank.

To do something about Frank's tension, Catherine needs more specific information. For starters: what happened recently that made Frank complain about the customer service department?

But first, she needs to get a feeling where Frank is in his grieving process regarding Hans. She heard that Frank was the customer service agent who was closest to Hans. How close, she doesn't know. But she knows that for Frank to open up to her (the first step to attach and bond), he needs to have had enough opportunity to separate from Hans and grieve. She also knows that going through these phases is different for each person. Since it's hard for her to predict what is necessary for Frank, she decides to ask him.

"Frank, can I ask you a question?"

"OK," Frank answers in a reserved manner.

"What kind of relationship did you have with Hans?" Catherine asks.

"We got along rather well. I saw the effort he made for the team and appreciated it, unlike most others."

"So, I assume you feel bad that he is at home now. Is that correct?" asks Catherine.

"I hope he gets better soon," states Frank, "but, to be honest, I don't think he was the best person to lead this team, despite his efforts and good intentions."

When Catherine hears this, she guesses that Frank's grieving period is already over or at least in the last stage. She knows she still has to be careful but decides to change the direction of the conversation.

"From what I hear, it's important to you that a manager makes a deliberate effort to help their team. Is that correct?"

"Yes, that's correct," answers Frank.

"Well, I heard you say something about bad communication from the marketing department. It seems to have an impact on your work. I would like to offer my support to change this situation, so it doesn't bother you anymore. Is that OK with you?"

Frank is surprised by Catherine's offer. The unwritten law in the customer service department is that you're on your own and should solve any problems yourself. Asking others for help had been a dreadful experience for all of the team members. And now somebody proactively offers to help? That's something different. The first thought that comes up in Frank's mind is: "What does she want from me? What hidden agenda does she have?" But when he thinks about it, he can't come up with anything. So he decides to give it a cautious try.

"OK," Frank answers.

"What happened that made you say that the communication of the marketing department is bad?" Catherine asks.

"The e-mail from marketing about the launch of the new external hard drives was bad," Frank vents. "Just like their e-mail about the promotion with the USB sticks. They don't know what they're talking about and I have to deal with all the complaints. I assume it was George who hired those marketing folks since he is the manager of that team. He doesn't have a clue what he is doing. He should be fired."

Catherine listens and analyzes Frank's answer. It shows her a few things:

- Frank has been experiencing tension for a while.
- It still isn't clear to her what the problem is.
- Frank makes an entanglement of several tensions. There seems to be practical tension (the e-mails), personal tension (dealing with the complaints) and interpersonal tension (blaming the marketing department and suggesting that George should be fired).
- It's not clear what Frank wants or how Catherine can support him.

Catherine realizes that if she wants to support Frank, she needs to separate the threads and focus on one. She knows that the best way to do this, is to utilize a compassionate attitude. And that the framework that can be used is a four-step process called the D.U.E.T. process.

The D.U.E.T. Process

The D.U.E.T. process is a framework I have developed to transform tension, taking the specific vibes into account.

D.U.E.T. is an acronym that stands for:
- Detect and face the tension.
- Understand and solve the tension.
- Embrace and transform the root of the tension.
- Take action.

This process can be used in any situation where a tension emerges. It can be applied by an individual that identifies a tension (on his own), by a leader who is coaching a team member, by a manager who is facilitating a team during a meeting, or by a coach who is working with a client or with group of trainees.

Here is a short visual representation of the D.U.E.T. process, including the tools and techniques that can be used in each step.

D.U.E.T. Process

1. Detect and face the tension		
2. Understand and solve the tension		
Interpersonal tension	Practical tension	Personal tension
Compassion Technique	Compassionate Problem Solving	The ABCs of De-stressing
3. Embrace and transform the root of the tension		
Compassion Quadrants	Compassionate Problem Solving	Inner Balance Technique
4. Take action		
Compassionate Communication	Apply the Proposal	Self Care

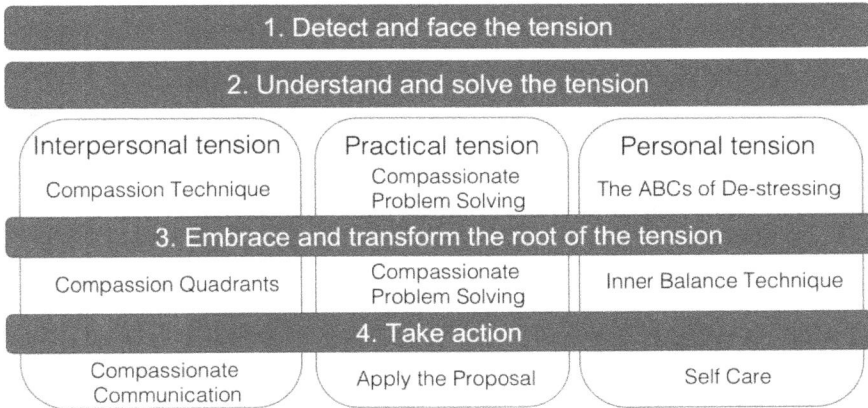

As you read in chapter 3, Compassionate Leaders are balanced people. This means a balance between mind, heart, and body, a balance between masculine and feminine qualities and a balance between the conscious and the unconscious.

You will see this reflected in these techniques. If you have always lived your life from a primarily rational or mental approach, some of these techniques can seem a little strange at first. But when you've read the explanation afterward, it will become clear why the techniques are constructed this way. I invite you to try out the techniques and experience for yourself what they can do for you. And if you're like me, you'll probably skip them while reading the book for the first time. That's perfectly fine. Come back to them later.

In the next four chapters, you will be guided through the four steps of the D.U.E.T. process. Each step is dealt with in a separate chapter. In each chapter you will receive more insight into each step, an explanation of each tool and technique and why they are used.

When a tension shows up at work, and there is enough time, you can go through the four steps. This will yield the best results. However, sometimes, there isn't enough time or space to do this. Then you can skip steps. For example: when you detect a tension (step 1), you can use Compassionate Communication to enquire about it (step 4). In other words, the D.U.E.T. process is a flexible framework that can be used in any circumstance where tension is present.

The benefit of the D.U.E.T. process is not only about having the techniques to transform tensions; it also offers a reference frame and a common language. For example, when every team member knows the Compassion Quadrants technique, another team member might say: "I notice you keep having conflicts with our manager. Why don't we use the Compassion Quadrants to find out what it is really about?" Or before or during a meeting, the person who is leading it can say: "We all know this is a rather delicate subject. Let's all do the Compassion Technique first." The benefit is that there is less blaming, less defensiveness, more openness, faster transforming of tensions, and a quicker way to raise the vibe.

Key Take-Aways

To raise the vibe of an individual or a team, we can use the moments of tension. This is called "navigating by tension" and brings more clarity to a situation. When there is more clarity, there can be more compassion and more room to increase the vibe.

The process to deal with tensions is called the four-step D.U.E.T. process, or more poetically, performing a D.U.E.T. with tension.

D.U.E.T. is an acronym that stands for:

- Detect and face the tension.
- Understand and solve the tension.
- Embrace and transform the root of the tension.
- Take action.

The D.U.E.T process is a flexible framework that can be used when any tension (practical/process, personal or interpersonal) is detected. An extra benefit is that it provides a reference frame and a common language. This helps to raise the vibe quicker.

In the next four chapters, you will be guided through the four steps. Each step is dealt with in a separate chapter. In each chapter, you will receive more insights in each step of the D.U.E.T. process, instructions on how to apply the associated techniques and an explanation of why they are used.

Chapter 6

Detect and Face the Tension

D.U.E.T. Process

1. Detect and face the tension		
2. Understand and solve the tension		
Interpersonal tension Compassion Technique	Practical tension Compassionate Problem Solving	Personal tension The ABCs of De-stressing
3. Embrace and transform the root of the tension		
Compassion Quadrants	Compassionate Problem Solving	Inner Balance Technique
4. Take action		
Compassionate Communication	Apply the Proposal	Self Care

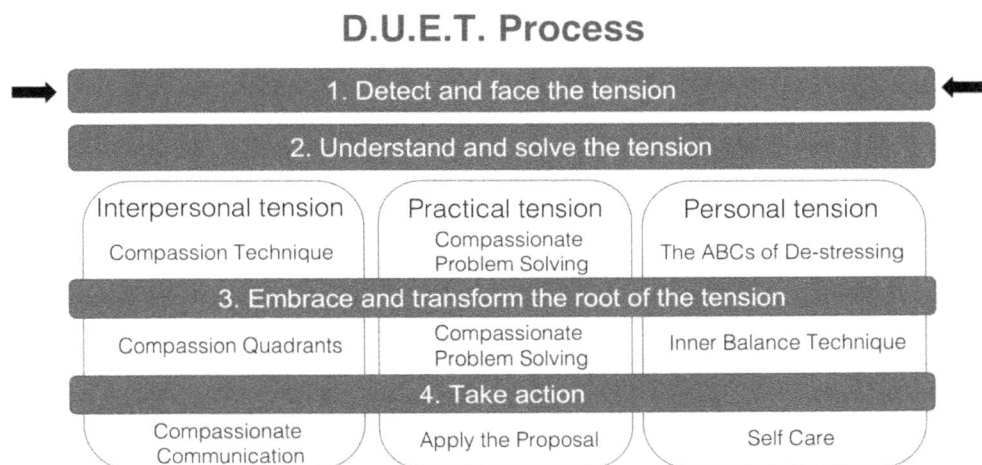

The first step in the D.U.E.T. process is acknowledging that there is tension. Don't ignore it, don't push it away, don't project it on something or someone else or don't use one of the coping strategies — blaming others, venting, micromanagement or suppressing the tension.

In the example where account manager Jeffrey feels tension about not acquiring enough customers, it's not about:
- Ignoring this tension and doing the same thing.
- Pushing it away and hoping that a change will occur spontaneously.
- Projecting it on something (bad economy) or someone (marketing is doing a bad job), and continuing to complain about external circumstances.

It's also not about hearing someone complain (like in the example of customer service agent Frank) and just let it pass. When someone complains, their unconscious goal is to get rid of some tension. The sooner this is detected, the less tensions can start to build up and get entangled.

So, it starts with detecting the tension and acknowledging its presence. This is not that hard to do. Just observe and listen to what people say. Some people literally point out the problem or opportunity for growth. Others do it indirectly, like via complaining and gossiping.

Detecting tension is not so difficult, but it's not always easy to *face* the tension. Facing tension requires willingness and courage. It's easy when people are in a positive or inspiring vibe. It's more difficult in a negative or neutral vibe.

On the level of practical tensions, facing them requires a willingness to change. Change means going into unknown territories and leaving something behind. Even when the old situation was not ideal (or just bad), many people fear the unknown even more. That's why they might refuse to look at tension, especially when they don't feel safe (negative or neutral vibe) or not encouraged (positive or inspiring vibe).

On the level of personal or interpersonal tensions, facing it might require changing your perspective or looking at your weaknesses, shadow sides, or fears. They might show up during the process. In reality, sometimes they show up, and sometimes they don't. But the fear of *potentially* having to change an opinion or face a weakness, makes many people avoid this step.

That's why it's so important to have someone with the skills and attitude of a Compassionate Leader to facilitate this process in the early stages. When all team members are familiar with the techniques, they can go through the steps on their own or facilitate each other.

Conditions to Face Tension

The D.U.E.T. process can be done individually, with a partner (colleague, manager, internal or external coach) or with a group.

Since it can be more challenging to face tension with a partner or with a group of people, most of the techniques are designed in a way that tension can be solved without having to describe the situation or naming the other people involved. This creates safety. As a consequence, it's much easier to face tension.

However, for some tensions (especially practical ones) or at some later stage in the process, it can be necessary to voice what the tension is about. To make this as safe and constructive as possible, there are guidelines. I suggest you voice them every time you use the D.U.E.T. process.

For a person who is detecting the tension, here are the guidelines:
- This is your time and space.
- Share what feels right, nothing more, nothing less.
- If anybody asks you a personal question that you don't want to answer, you can respectfully say "no." It's OK to keep the answer to yourself.
- This is a moment for solving your tension, so you're no longer bothered by it (negative tension) or can benefit from the opportunity (positive tension). This process could start with getting things off your chest, but you need to be willing to take the next step.

For a partner or group members:
- Hold the space for the person who detects the tension.
- If appropriate, use a talking stick.
- Ask for permission when you want to ask a question or want to offer a suggestion.

Let's dive a bit deeper in what these three guidelines for the partner or group members mean.

Holding space

Holding space for someone is a simple but powerful action. Actually, it's not really an action. It's about being with someone without saying anything. This way, you can hold space for someone to go through the D.U.E.T. process.

It teaches us that just being with someone is often enough. We don't have to come up with solutions all the time. It also teaches us to focus on someone else, to give someone else space and time. As a result, we can let ourselves off the hook. We don't have to be the savior. It's very respectful and compassionate to just be with someone. Only go into solution or action mode when they ask for it.

Holding space also means that you *keep* the focus on someone else. If something happens with you during the process, you can write it down, but don't share it with the other person or with the group.

One of the aspects of going through the D.U.E.T. process together is that the person detecting a tension may feel that they're getting all the time and space necessary. This is something that not many people experience in their daily lives. And usually receiving all the time and space, doesn't take much time at all.

Talking stick

The goal of the talking stick is that only the person who holds the stick is allowed to speak. All other people are silent until they have the talking stick in their hand. Whenever someone is done speaking, they put the talking stick back in the middle of the group.

In the D.U.E.T. process, the person who detected the tension is the first one to hold the talking stick. When that person is finished and puts the talking stick back in the middle of the group, someone else can pick it up and speak. In some D.U.E.T. processes, only the person who detected a tension that is only applicable to them (like a personal tension) gets to speak. The holding space of the group might be enough for them to go through the four steps.

A talking stick can be a great tool when working with a group of people who are constantly interrupting each other. A talking stick creates respectful conversation. Especially in this kind of process of dealing with tension, it is important that feedback or advice is shared in a serene way. It also gives more space to introverted people who need more time to formulate a question or a suggestion.

You can use any item you want as a talking stick. Just make sure that every group member knows that the item is the only talking stick during the session.

Ask for permission

One of the subtler uncompassionate actions is sharing unsolicited advice. It crosses boundaries and creates extra (interpersonal) tension for people.

What happens a lot in traditional meetings is that the meeting has been organized to solve a practical issue, but that people leave frustrated by the behavior of some participants (and many times without a decent solution).

Asking for permission to share an idea or question, whether or not during a meeting, is a respectful and compassionate gesture. Even if you are using a talking stick, it's still important to ask for permission before sharing any advice or feedback with the person who detected the tension. It gives the signal that you want to treat them with respect.

How to Detect Tension

Let's go back to detecting tension. What are the ways to do so?

When you stop running around, sit down and get your mind off your to-do list, tensions present themselves rather quickly.

Here are a few examples:

Customer complaints. Whenever there is a customer complaint, there is tension. The tension increases when the same complaints keep coming back. So, it's important to look at the cause of the tension between what the organization does and what the customers want. Maybe it's about the products or the process, but it can also point to a changing marketplace with new opportunities.

Customer requests also point to those new opportunities. They are a kind of tension as well.

Besides those external factors, there are similar internal ones. **Complaints or requests by other departments, teams, or colleagues** can also be triggers for tension.

In general, an easy way of detecting tension is to hear what someone (including yourself) is **complaining** about. When people complain, they want to get rid of tension. However, it's a temporary solution. Only when performing a D.U.E.T. it can be transformed. In other words, I invite you to shift your perception about complaining from now on. Consider it as the start of a transformation, instead of bad behavior from negative people. Be grateful for the complainers!

Our **body** can be a very good indicator of tension as well. It can be about a spot that aches permanently or occasionally. For many people, tension comes up in your body when you think of a person or a situation. This may happen in your stomach, but it can also manifest itself in the throat region or other parts of the body. This can be a contracting feeling (fear or negative tension) or an expanding feeling (joy or positive tension).

As a side note, HSPs (Highly Sensitive People) feel tensions intensely. Their contribution to detecting tensions can be invaluable, like a canary in a coal mine. Companies that want to grow and change could make better use of their HSPs by asking them which tensions they are picking upon. In most organizations, this is not the case. The result is that HSPs are at home suffering from burnout, which can cost the company a lot of money (since they can't stop feeling the tensions anyway and are overwhelmed by them). Asking HSPs about potential tensions helps to detect problems. The benefit is that problems are tackled right away (before they start growing) and opportunities are spotted sooner. Tapping into the sensory talents of HSPs is not currently happening in the workplace. But in a world where companies are always looking for the next competitive advantage, this could be one of the areas that will help.

Gizmo Objects Inc.

In customer service agent Frank's case, it would have been easy for his manager Catherine to ignore his comment about bad communication in the company.

However, she knows that a complaint points to a tension. It starts by enquiring what is going on from a compassionate attitude. It's about being open and curious while keeping her opinions and prejudices to herself. Catherine knows that focusing on Frank and being fully present will be very important in solving his tension and raising his vibe.

This will make Frank feel safe enough to give a few more details regarding his comments about the e-mails, customer complaints, and firing George.

It's clear to Catherine that this situation is seriously bothering Frank and has been bothering him for a long time. Frank seems to be in a negative vibe. Catherine knows that when people are ignored, it's normal to end up in a negative vibe. So, she doesn't judge him for that.

She knows that to transform the tensions Frank is experiencing, she needs to take his current vibe into account. She has to offer enough safety and security to go a step deeper and detect which tensions are at play. Holding the space for Frank and asking him for permission to explore what is going on, are crucial first steps in starting the D.U.E.T. process. She knows she has to hold her advice and solutions to herself — at least for now. Later on in the process, there may be a need or opportunity to offer advice. For now, she holds off. She also knows that a talking stick can be useful, but not necessary in the current informal setting. She decides that she will pay attention to how Frank expresses himself and seek permission whenever she feels the need to ask a question or share something.

Once a tension is detected and a safe environment has been created, and once there is enough willingness to look at the tension, we can go to the next step of the D.U.E.T. process in the next chapter: understanding and solving the tension.

Key Take-Aways

The first step of the D.U.E.T. process entails being aware of the tension and being willing to look at it.

Detecting tensions is not so hard. These are a few ways:
- Customer complaints.
- Customer requests.
- Complaints or requests by other departments, teams, or colleagues.
- Signals of your body.

Facing tension requires courage.

A safe environment supports this, along with some guidelines like holding space, using a talking stick and asking for permission. Just like facilitation by someone who has the capacities of a Compassionate Leader.

Chapter 7

Understand and Solve the Tension

D.U.E.T. Process

1. Detect and face the tension		
2. Understand and solve the tension		
Interpersonal tension Compassion Technique	Practical tension Compassionate Problem Solving	Personal tension The ABCs of De-stressing
3. Embrace and transform the root of the tension		
Compassion Quadrants	Compassionate Problem Solving	Inner Balance Technique
4. Take action		
Compassionate Communication	Apply the Proposal	Self Care

The second step of the D.U.E.T. process is about understanding and solving the tension.

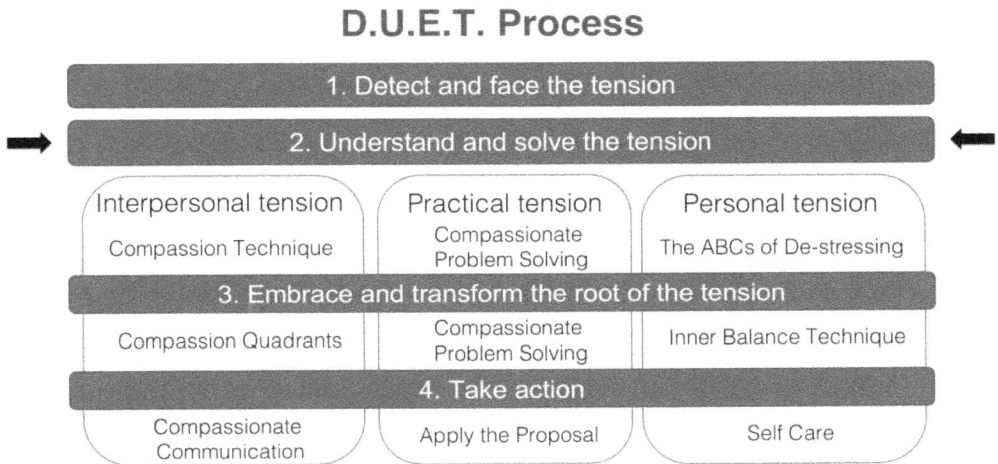

Understanding the tension means placing it in one of the three categories of tension. Then the appropriate technique can be used to *solve* it.

As a reminder, these are the three categories of tension:

- **Practical or process tension**: the order and shipping processes are not optimally aligned, data input takes a long time since it's done manually, meetings take forever because there is no structured approach, co-workers are constantly sick because of open doors or malfunctioning air-conditioning systems.
- **Personal tension**: I don't feel able to do what is expected of me, I have low self-esteem, I feel resistance to change, I hate public speaking.
- **Interpersonal tension**: I don't get along with a colleague, manager, customer, supplier; I have fights with them or feel uncomfortable in their company.

In the workplace, certain causes of tension involve practical issues. Many times, a practical solution is enough to transform the tension.

However, when tension on a practical level becomes mixed up with tension on a personal or interpersonal level, it becomes much more difficult to look at. In the example of customer service agent Frank, you see that the result is to ignore the tensions to maintain the status quo.

So, the first step is to put the tension in one of the above categories. If the tension involves more than one category, break it down into several sub-tensions.

Once you understand to which category a tension belongs, you can use the appropriate technique or tool to solve it. The main ones we use, are:

- To solve interpersonal tension: The Compassion Technique.
- To solve practical or process tension: Compassionate Problem Solving.
- To solve personal tension: The ABCs of De-stressing.

Solving Interpersonal Tension: The Compassion Technique

It isn't always easy to face tension or to look for the root of a tension when you have a conflict with one or more of the people involved. Or when you don't feel enough freedom or safety to voice your opinion or suggestions. The reason could be a dominant CEO or co-worker. But it could also be someone you consider weak or someone you don't want to burden.

To change this situation, I have created the Compassion Technique. It is a technique that combines several aspects:
- Stress release
- Balancing relationships
- Optimal brain usage

It's both the perfect *preparation* for the whole D.U.E.T. process (to feel more safe and open for a change) and an excellent way to *solve interpersonal tensions*.

Purpose of the Compassion Technique

For the *individual*, there are many circumstances and purposes to use the Compassion Technique:

- Experience compassion, inner peace, and balance within 10 to 15 minutes;
- Carry less emotions from previous experience into the next one;
- Be more open towards the other person in the future;
- Notice solutions when you got stuck;
- Have fulfilling conversations and relationships;
- See more possibilities regarding a specific situation;
- Grow as a person;
- Raise your consciousness;
- Feel more freedom in your life.

If the Compassion Technique and the D.U.E.T. process are used by a *team*, the team will become more harmonious, more efficient, and more effective.

Starting point

Most people start using the Compassion Technique when they feel limited by someone else in some way, when they have a conflict with someone, when they don't have a balanced relationship with another person or when they feel they need to get more centered before a meeting or facilitating a group. In other words, the technique is helpful in a situation where there is (potential) tension with other people.

The other people can be anybody: a CEO, manager, co-worker, customer, supplier, or any other professional. You can also apply it with anybody else in your mind: your spouse, children, parents, neighbor, or any other person in your life.

Here are some examples when the Compassion Technique can help a team member:

- He has a heated argument with a colleague about whose responsibility it is to communicate a negative result to a customer.
- She doesn't feel appreciated by the CEO or another manager for the work she does.

- He cringes when the CEO or another team member voices the smallest bit of criticism.
- She feels hurt when the CEO only reads the first page of a 50-page report she compiled.
- He feels small and vulnerable in a team meeting, especially when one specific person talks or is present.
- She feels pressured by a customer to lower the price below a healthy margin.
- He must go into a meeting with someone he has previously argued with or with someone who creates tension.
- She feels sad and afraid because a co-worker bullies her.
- He feels frustrated because a supplier doesn't listen to his requests to modify the product specifications.
- She is being screamed at by an unsatisfied customer.

Gizmo Objects Inc.

Catherine notices that one of Frank's complaints is about the marketing department and marketing manager George. She knows that interpersonal tensions usually block solutions for any issue. That's why she decides to start with those tensions.

"Frank, can I ask you a question about the marketing department?" asks Catherine.

The question seems to wake Frank up from his rant about everything that is going wrong.

"Yeah, sure," he answers.

"How do you feel about them?" Catherine asks.

"Well, they are a bunch of incompetent people that make my life miserable," Frank responds.

"Well, it sounds like they give you a lot of stress," Catherine says.

"That's right," Frank answers.

"Are you interested in learning a technique that will reduce the stress you get from the marketing team?" asks Catherine.

"I'm not sure that will help," responds Frank.

"Are you willing to give it a try?" asks Catherine. "It might also help you deal with stress that you get from other people, both at work and home."

"OK, let's try this technique of yours," Frank answers.

To Catherine, he still seems to be a bit reluctant, but also open to giving it a try. She knows that's enough for now.

"Let's go to the next room, where it is quieter and where we can close the door," suggests Catherine.

She knows that this helps to create a safe environment. Frank agrees and follows her.

"The technique I referred to is the Compassion Technique," Catherine explains. "It helps to reduce the stress you get from other people. It is a technique you can do on your own but it is easier when someone else guides you through the steps. An extra benefit of the Compassion Technique is that you don't have to tell anyone about the situation."

Without the eyes of his colleagues resting on him, Frank already feels a bit safer. Catherine seems to be OK as well. Although she has only recently become his manager and he doesn't know her very well, she seems to have respect for all employees, whatever function or role they have. She also doesn't seem to want to push her agenda. This is nice because it doesn't create any more tensions between team members. It feels a bit weird that she suggests using a technique to lower the stress he gets from other people. But maybe it will also help him to better deal with his son, who is going through puberty. This creates lots of friction in the family. The technique also feels safe enough because everything remains anonymous.

"OK, I'm ready for it," Frank answers.

Catherine smiles, pulls up the instructions she downloaded from the Compassionate Leader website, and leads Frank through the steps.

The process takes 18 minutes, which is a bit longer than usual. Catherine knows that this can happen when an individual is going through it for the very first time. She also knows that the more frequently people use it, the faster it goes.

"Well, how are you feeling now?" Catherine asks.

"Wow, much better," Frank answers. "I feel much more at ease. I also realize that the person who was stressing me out isn't all that bad."

Catherine is pleased to hear this but is not surprised. This is the usual effect. She is also glad to see that Frank's vibe is shifting. He doesn't seem to be in a negative vibe anymore, but more in a neutral vibe. She is happy because she knows she can now work with Frank to look at his other tensions.

The Compassion Technique

As you read in Frank and Catherine's story, the Compassion Technique can be done alone or with someone else. It's easier if someone else reads the instructions, so you can focus on what's happening. You can do this exercise with a coach or a co-worker you trust. You can also use the free video that I created as a guide (see the Training Center on the website). As a leader or a coach, you can facilitate an individual or a group by leading them through the steps.

A huge benefit of using the Compassion Technique is that 95 percent is done in silence. The person who is going through the steps of the Compassion Technique also doesn't have to share any details. This creates safety.

That's why we start with this technique when working with a person or a team with their center of gravity in a negative vibe. The Compassion Technique helps them to shift to a neutral vibe easily. Once they are in a neutral vibe, it is easier to focus on solutions for other tensions.

The Compassion Technique is a procedure that combines different short techniques to bring forward the best result. Some of these short techniques draw upon rational capacities, others upon visual and bodily senses. As explained before, it is the combination that often gets the best results, instead of a unilateral cognitive or physical approach.

In the next parts you will first be presented with the instructions. Then there is a short explanation of the lesser-known techniques that are part of the Compassion Technique.

The Compassion Technique: Instructions

Before you start with the Compassion Technique, take a notepad and a pen. You can use them to write down insights during or after applying the technique.

Note: At first glance, this may seem like a long process, but that's because there are a few iterations built-in that can be used or skipped over depending on the situation. The main process consists of only 10 steps.

1. Remember a recent situation at work or in your private life, with one other person involved, where you felt a lot of tension. You felt resentful, frustrated, angry or quite irritated by the behavior of the other person. This could be a colleague, boss, fellow employee, customer, supplier or business partner. Or it could be your (ex-) partner, child, parent, family member, neighbor, club member, …

2. Rate this tension with a number from 0 to 10, with 0 being no tension at all and 10 is feeling completely overwhelmed by tension.
   Note: it's only useful to do this regarding situations where the number is higher than 3. When lower, you should be able to deal with the situation.

3. Close your eyes. Visualize the other person. For some people this will be an image, others will rather feel or hear it.
   a. Where is this other person located? In front of you, behind you, to the left, to the right, at an angle? How far away does this person stand and whereabout does he or she stand compared to you? What do you see, what do you hear, what do you feel, what do you smell or what do you taste?
   b. How tall is he or she? And how tall are you?
   c. If you can perceive it: how is his or her facial expression? Angry, frustrated, neutral, happy…? How is your facial expression?
   d. Open your eyes when you have the image.

4. Name the tension. Which word would you attach to it? Which emotion or which feeling? What is the main feeling and emotion in yourself?

5. Sit on a chair.
    a. Sit in the Whole Brain Position: cross your ankles, right over left and place your feet underneath the chair so they touch the ground (see image below). Keep your arms stretched out in front of you, parallel to the ground and with your palms outwards. Cross your wrists, left over right and interlock your fingers. Put your hands in your lap or roll them further up until they rest on your chest.
    b. Close your eyes.
    c. Breathe in and out deeply three times.
    d. Imagine there's a little golden ball above your head. Imagine it is sinking through the top of your head, in the center. Imagine it keeps sinking further, behind your eyes, behind your nose and through your mouth, through your throat down to your chest, until it gets to your heart. Keep the little ball there and also focus your attention there.
    e. Remain like this for a minute or so, until you feel you are relaxed or until your eyes automatically open, followed up by putting your arms and legs back into a neutral position.

Whole Brain Position

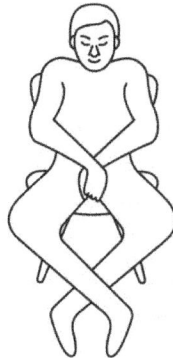

6. Think back of the situation and answer the questions below in your mind (or you can write the answers down if you want). Close your eyes and just be with the question for about 30 seconds, even if the answer will come to you immediately. Reflect or feel if there's something else coming up. *Sometimes rational answers will pop up, sometimes just a feeling and sometimes nothing will happen. Whatever happens, it's OK. If you don't get any answer, continue with the next question or step.*

a. "What is the underlying need of the other person, beyond the behavior?"

b. "Which assumptions did I make in this situation? And when I look back at those assumptions, are they really true?"

c. "How would I react if I knew that the other person had received some bad news that morning (sick child, parent passed away, being fired,…)?"

7. Reflect on your answers. Check if you gained insights in the other person, in yourself or in your relationship. If you want, you can write down the answers, insights or questions.

8. Close your eyes. Visualize the other person again and see if there are differences compared to the previous visualization.

a. Where is this other person located? In front of you, behind you, to the left, to the right, at an angle? How far away does this person stand and whereabout does he or she stand compared to you? What do you see, what do you hear, what do you feel, what do you smell or what do you taste?

b. How tall is he or she? And how tall are you?

c. If you can perceive it: how is his or her facial expression? Angry, frustrated, neutral, happy…? How is your facial expression?

d. Open your eyes when you have the image.

9. Go back to your initial emotion. Rate it again on a scale of 0 to 10.

a. Did it change?

b. If it is below 3, go to step 22.

10. Think back of the situation and answer these questions in your mind (or you can write the answers down if you want):

a. "What was the trigger for the behavior of the other person in this situation?"

b. "What if this person (unconsciously) protected something that was valuable to them? And what could that be?"

c. "What do I wish for the other person?"

11. Reflect on your answers. Check if you gained insights in the other person, in yourself or in your relationship. If you want, you can write down the answers, insights or questions.

12. Close your eyes. Visualize the other person again and see if there are differences compared to the previous visualization.
    a. Where is this other person located? In front of you, behind you, to the left, to the right, at an angle? How far away does this person stand and whereabout does he or she stand compared to you? What do you see, what do you hear, what do you feel, what do you smell or what do you taste?
    b. How tall is he or she? And how tall are you?
    c. If you can perceive it: how is his or her facial expression? Angry, frustrated, neutral, happy…? How is your facial expression?
    d. Open your eyes when you have the image.

13. Go back to your initial emotion. Rate it again on a scale of 0 to 10.
    a. Did it change?
    b. If it is below 3, go to step 22.

14. Think back of the situation and answer these questions in your mind (or you can write the answers down if you want):
    a. "What was NOT said in this situation? Which underlying tension was not addressed?"
    b. "What did I do, consciously or unconsciously, that has contributed to this situation?"
    c. "Why was the behavior of the other person in that situation the best way to take care of themselves?"

15. Reflect on your answers. Check if you gained insights in the other person, in yourself or in your relationship. If you want, you can write down the answers, insights or questions.

16. Close your eyes. Visualize the other person again and see if there are differences compared to the previous visualization.
    a. Where is this other person located? In front of you, behind you, to the left, to the right, at an angle? How far away does this person stand and whereabout does he or she stand compared to you? What do you see, what do you hear, what do you feel, what do you smell or what do you taste?
    b. How tall is he or she? And how tall are you?
    c. If you can perceive it: how is his or her facial expression? Angry, frustrated, neutral, happy…? How is your facial expression?
    d. Open your eyes when you have the image.

17. Go back to your initial emotion. Rate it again on a scale of 0 to 10.
    a. Did it change?
    b. If it is below 3, go to step 22.

18. Think back of the situation and answer these questions in your mind (or you can write the answers down if you want):
    a. "What would happen if I postponed my opinion or judgment regarding this situation?"
    b. "Do I know the real needs and boundaries of the other person regarding the situation?"
    c. "What other path towards happiness than mine is the other person pursuing?"

19. Reflect on your answers. Check if you gained insights in the other person, in yourself or in your relationship. If you want, you can write down the answers, insights or questions.

20. Close your eyes. Visualize the other person again and see if there are differences compared to the previous visualization.
    a. Where is this other person located? In front of you, behind you, to the left, to the right, at an angle? How far away does this person stand and whereabout does he or she stand compared to you? What do you see, what do you hear, what do you feel, what do you smell or what do you taste?
    b. How tall is he or she? And how tall are you?
    c. If you can perceive it: how is his or her facial expression? Angry, frustrated, neutral, happy...? How is your facial expression?
    d. Open your eyes when you have the image.

21. Go back to your initial emotion. Rate it again on a scale of 0 to 10.
    a. Did it change?
    b. If it is below 3, go to step 22. *In the exceptional case that the tension is not below 3, notice what did change. For some people going from a 9 to a 5 already makes a huge difference. Sometimes that's enough for the time being. In other cases an extra round can be useful. For the scope of the book the number of rounds is limited to four. On the website you can find an online kit that includes cards with questions. You can use them for the extra rounds.*

22. Last phase.
    a. Get back into sitting in the Whole Brain Position. Close your eyes. Cross your ankles, right over left and place your feet underneath the chair so they touch the ground. Keep your arms stretched out in front of you, parallel to the ground and with your palms outwards. Cross your wrists, left over right and interlock your fingers. Put your hands in your lap or roll them further up until they rest on your chest.
    b. What is the feeling which has replaced the initial emotion?
    c. Feel this new feeling regarding this person in that situation.
    d. Unlock your ankles when you have completely felt this feeling through.
    e. Unlock your wrists and put your finger tips against one another (left thumb against right thumb, left index finger against right index finger, etc.) press them against each other for about 10 seconds while you are in contact with this new feeling.
    f. While you continue pressing your fingertips against each other and keep staying in contact with this new feeling, you open your eyes. Look at your fingertips for 10 seconds and release them afterwards.

Whole Brain Position

110

Background information about the Compassion Technique

You might have some questions about the Compassion Technique. Let's look at the two parts that are new or not generally used by most people: the Whole Brain Position and visualizations.

Whole Brain Position

It may feel weird to assume the Whole Brain Position. So, let's explain why we use this technique and why it is beneficial.

The Whole Brain Position was devised by learning specialist Paul Dennison. The reason why we assume this position is that an emotional attachment leads to below-par decisions and that emotions block parts of our brain. With the Whole Brain Position, we get full access to our brain again.

Whenever we experience stress, parts of our brain are activated, and other parts are muted, silenced or disconnected. In other words, we don't have the full capacity to deal with a situation anymore, and that overwhelms us even more.

How does this show?

Option 1: We go into feeling mode only. We don't have access to practical solutions anymore. To others, it seems like we are running around like a chicken with its head cut off. We get stuck in emotions. This disconnection from the parts in our brain that are responsible for taking action happens a lot to women.

Option 2: We go into rational mode only. We don't have access to our emotional side anymore. To others, it feels cold and distant. This disconnection from the parts in our brain that are responsible for connecting with others happens a lot to men.

You will find a deeper explanation about what happens in stress situations a bit further in this chapter in the section about solving personal tension.

The action of having your limbs cross over the central meridian of your body during the Whole Brain Position connects the two hemispheres of our brain and reconnects the rational and emotional parts.

Performing the Whole Brain Position is very easy. I invite you to use it whenever you feel stress of any kind. You can do it very quickly on the toilet or in situations where you don't have time to do the whole Compassion Technique routine. The Whole Brain Position will instantly help you to release stress and be more centered. This will help deal with the situation and have access to more options and solutions.

Visualizations

Visualizations can be a great aid. No wonder pro athletes use some kind of visualization to increase their performance.

However, some people are better at visualizing than others. Other people don't see anything but feel the images in some way. That's also OK. If visualizing or using any other senses doesn't work for you at all, no worries. The main goal of the visualization is that the images you see are an extra aid in feeling the progress that you make. When you notice that the other person is in another position or has changed in height, you know that you are making progress. But putting a number on the level of tension is just as good.

The specific visualization of the small golden ball helps us to calm further down (after sitting in the Whole Brain Position and taking three breaths) and experience a centered stance.

For some people, recalling the peaceful image at the end of the Compassion Technique can also help to be more centered and at peace when meeting that person again.

In short, visualization is an extra aid that can be beneficial, but don't worry if you or the person you are facilitation don't see any images.

Free video, PDF and FAQ

There is a video of the Compassion Technique available in the free section of the Training Center at www.thecompassionateleader.org

In the video, I take you through the steps, so you don't have to read them from a page or ask anybody to assist you. In the video, I draw cards from a deck instead of using a fixed format. That's hard to simulate in a book, so that's why you were presented with this fixed sequence above.

The website also offers answers to frequently asked questions about the Compassion Technique plus a PDF with instructions.

Solving Practical or Process Tension: Compassionate Problem Solving

In the workplace, most of the tensions are about practical issues. However, when they are not dealt with in the right way, they have the tendency to create interpersonal tensions. When that happens, it is usually necessary to deal with the interpersonal tension first before there is room to solve the practical tension. This is what Catherine did with Frank.

For now, let's assume we are only dealing with a practical tension. When a practical tension is detected, people don't always have a good method at their disposal to solve it.

In many cases, teams use meetings to find solutions. However, the traditional structure and approach of meetings are not designed to get the best results. On the contrary, they often cause extra interpersonal tensions.

One of the patterns in traditional meetings is that the dominant people or manager makes the decision, whether or not they are experts. Or the opposite happens: everybody needs to agree before an action can be taken, whether or not they know anything about the topic at hand (consensus). This is often linked to endless discussions and too many participants, and 80 percent of the group wondering why they were invited in the first place.

Usually, only a few of the topics on the agenda are discussed during the meeting. The rest is moved to the next meeting or isn't discussed at all. As a result, tensions aren't dealt with, or they are left to be solved by individuals (who get criticized later because they took no action or the wrong one).

One way to deal with these issues is by using a structured process. Such processes are situated in the heart of self-regulating models like Holacracy and Sociocracy 3.0 (S3). The good news is that parts of those models can be used by any team, whether it's self-regulating or not.

By using a structured process that is equal for all parties involved, many personal and interpersonal tensions don't get the chance to grow. Dominant bosses or co-workers don't receive more time or influence than others. Extraverted people don't get the chance to digress or speak more than introverted people. And there are no endless and frustrating discussions.

The process that we use is called Compassionate Problem Solving. It's used to solve practical tensions and borrows several elements from S3. It's a way of dealing with practical tensions from a true compassionate mindset.

Here are the three elements that make up the core of Compassionate Problem Solving:
- Formulate a Driver Statement
- Create a Proposal
- Apply Consent Decision-Making (agreeing on the proposal)

The next steps about formulating a driver statement, creating a proposal and agreeing upon the proposal using consent decision-making are based upon the information from *Sociocracy 3.0, a Practical Guide* by James Priest, Bernhard Bockelbrink and Liliana David. You can download it for free from www.sociocracy30.org (CC BY-SA 4.0 license).

Formulate a driver statement

In S3, the phrase "navigate via tension to discover a driver" is used. I like this terminology since it shows that any tension, whether we perceive it as negative or positive, can drive an individual, team, or organization forward.

The *driver* sums up what the tension is about. A simple way to describe a driver is with a brief statement explaining:

- What's happening:
  - the current situation
  - the effect of this situation on the organization (or individual or team)
- And what's needed:
  - the need of the organization about this situation
  - the impact of attending to that need

The driver statement contains just enough information to communicate the need for an action or decision. Typically, a driver statement can be summed up in one or two sentences.

Let's look at an example.

> "In the last three promotion e-mails, the customer service number was not the right one. This leads to customers dialing the wrong number,

being put on hold and yelling at customer service agents because they are frustrated from the long wait. We need better alignment between the marketing department and the customer service department to have satisfied customers and increase the NPS (Net Promoter Score)."

The first benefit of the driver statement is that it enforces reflection about the tension at hand: what is the tension about and what is the impact?

The second benefit is that it points to a direction for a practical solution (a proposal). This avoids just complaining about situations that cause tension.

The third benefit is that the statement is objective. It doesn't blame anyone. This avoids creating or renewing interpersonal tensions.

Create a proposal

After the driver statement has been formulated, a proposal that contains a practical solution can be created.

There are many ways to create or co-create proposals. They typically follow a similar pattern:

1. Agree on the driver.
2. Explore the topic and understand constraints.
3. Generate ideas.
4. Design a proposal (often done by an individual or a smaller group).

In Sociocracy3.0, the format of the proposal looks like this:
- Driver.
- Who is responsible for what?
- Description.
- Evaluation Process and Criteria.

Apply consent decision-making

After the proposal has been created, the solution can be put into practice.

In most cases, this is easier in theory than in reality. The reason is that the solution for most tensions is not the (sole) responsibility of the person who experiences the tension.

In traditional approaches, the best solution isn't always chosen. The solution tends to be backed by the most dominant people or is reached by consensus. This often creates more interpersonal tension on the one hand and doesn't solve the real cause of the practical tension on the other.

A rather new and much more efficient approach is consent-based, used in methodologies like Sociocracy3.0 (S3).

The definition of consent in this context is the absence of argued and paramount objections from those affected by a decision. The aim here is to quickly arrive at decisions that are good enough for now and safe enough to try. They don't need to be perfect. Consent is the absence of objections, not a consensus with unanimity. There is also no traditional group discussion, which allows for fast approval of proposals.

The benefits of consent decision-making are:

- Everyone's needs will be considered. Not everyone gets what they want, but every objection can be heard and addressed.
- More buy-in from all participants. No one leaves the room feeling disengaged.
- No negative behavior after the meeting. Consent is an active process. Everyone has to agree. Everyone in the room is equally responsible. There is no blaming others afterward.
- It saves time. Participants don't have to argue until they agree or one gives up. If there is no objection, participants consent. Any objections are dealt with.
- Objections give more information. Someone who votes "no" in a traditional setting may never explain why. In consent, participants harvest more information which can only be better for everyone. Objections are a gift.

As you can imagine, Compassionate Problem Solving is rather difficult when people are in a negative vibe. If that's the case, we use the Compassion Technique or The ABCs of De-stressing first. Once people are in a neutral vibe, Compassionate Problem Solving can be applied.

If Compassionate Problem Solving becomes the standard way of dealing with practical tensions, it also provides the way to transition to a positive vibe. This way of decision-making creates safety and inclusion (which prevents the vibe from going down) and emphasizes creating more ideas and solutions in a faster pace (which stimulates the vibe going up).

Gizmo Objects Inc.

After Catherine has guided Frank through the steps of the Compassion Technique, he is now more capable of looking at practical tensions. He is more at ease and less inclined to blame others. The interpersonal tension he felt was processed by using the Compassion Technique. Frank has shifted from a negative to a neutral vibe.

Catherine knows that people who just made this transition can easily fall back. She still needs to be a secure base for Frank. That's why she asks permission again to see whether or not it's a good moment to explore the practical tensions. Sometimes the right thing to do after the Compassion Technique is to have someone remain in this peaceful state (which is often rather new for people).

"Frank, are you willing to tell me more about the e-mails from the marketing department and why they cause you so much stress?" Catherine asks.

Frank reflects for a moment. He doesn't feel as much stress as before when thinking about the marketing department. Interesting. This Compassion Technique seems to work in some way.

"OK," Frank answers. "They always mix up the customer service numbers when they send out a marketing mail."

"I can imagine how that creates unnecessary tensions," Catherine responds. "But since I'm rather new here, I don't think I can grasp all the troubles it causes for our service department and maybe even other teams in the company. Can you share your insights with me?"

"Well, we have three different customer service numbers," explains Frank. "One number for each product line. When a customer calls a number, and there is no agent available, they are put on hold. When an agent becomes available, and they notice that it's for another product line, the customer is put through to the right number. Now, the customer can be put on hold again if there is no agent available."

"That must be annoying for the customer and hurts our NPS (Net Promoter Score)," says Catherine.

"Yes, but that is only part of the problem", explains Frank. "Whenever marketing announces a promotion, the service agents create a schedule to keep the waiting time to a minimum. This means that service agents of that specific product line work more hours a day and service agents from another product line take time off."

Frank continues: "The problem is that a customer who calls the wrong number ends up on hold since there are fewer service agents available for that number. And since there is a promotion going on, more customers call. So, the waiting time extends. Once they end up with the right service agent after they have been put through, they're usually furious because they had to wait so long. And that gives my colleagues and me a lot of unnecessary stress."

"Ah, I see," Catherine responds. "Has this information been shared with the marketing department?"

"Yes, or at least, we tried. But George, the manager of the marketing team, doesn't listen to us. He tells us we should be better organized. But when we explain that it's their fault, he gets angry and starts yelling."

For Catherine, this sounds like a classic example. When people start blaming each other, whether in a meeting or anywhere else, the other person goes in defense mode. Then it turns into protection oneself, their team, or their ideas. It becomes hard to listen to each other, detect what the real issue is, and find a solution.

"Would you be open to a different meeting format with the marketing team where the real issues are addressed without any shouting or emotional outbursts?" Catherine asks Frank.

"Is that possible?" Frank answers.

"Yes, if all participants are willing to follow a few guidelines and if you are willing to prepare the meeting with me." Catherine responds.

Frank reflects for a few moments. He likes the idea, and Catherine has been very supportive so far. But he still has some concerns.

"I don't think George will agree with the guidelines. If he doesn't agree with them, I don't want to be yelled at again," Frank responds.

"If George and all other participants agree to the guidelines, are you willing to participate?" Catherine asks.

"If you can give me that guarantee, I'm willing to give it a try," says Frank.

Catherine is happy with Frank's response. She notices the shift that Frank has made since the beginning of the conversation.

"OK! Thanks for your willingness," says Catherine. "I'll talk to George first and then come back to you to prepare for the meeting."

Five minutes later, Catherine is on the phone with George.

"George, I'm calling because there seems to be a misunderstanding between our departments. Can we set up a quick meeting to get that out of the way?"

"I think there is more than one misunderstanding between our departments," says George. "One meeting won't be enough. And I don't have time for any long meetings."

"I understand that you have a lot on your plate and dread long meetings," Catherine explains. "Are you open for an experiment? What if we could do a short meeting focused on one topic using a method that is called Compassionate Problem Solving? Maybe we don't only get this one topic solved, but you might also discover a method that can help eliminate any long meetings in the future."

"How long does the time slot need to be?" George asks.

"For this experiment, we need a maximum of 30 minutes," says Catherine. "But that implies that you have read the one-pager with guidelines upfront and agree to follow them."

George hesitates. He has held his meetings in the same way for the past 20 years and is not eager to change the format. He also doesn't like to be restricted by certain rules or guidelines. However, he admits that meetings sometimes take forever, and not everybody follows up on what has been agreed upon. The meetings also suck all the energy out of him and the other participants. If there is a good alternative, it might be helpful.

"E-mail me the guidelines, and I'll read them. If I like them, I'll send you a meeting request," George answers.

Catherine e-mails the guidelines right away. Two hours later she receives the request from George for a meeting the next day. Although she doesn't know George well, she was expecting him to agree. The guidelines make sense. It also sounded like he was tired of the problems between their departments. She goes over to Frank and shares that George is willing to follow the guidelines. In the meantime, Frank has also read the guidelines. He has become very interested in how the meeting will unfold and agrees to sit down with Catherine to prepare for it. They create a driver statement and a proposal.

The next day George, Catherine, Frank, and Ruben (a co-worker from the marketing team) meet at the agreed-upon time. Catherine asks if it's OK that she facilitates the meeting. Since she is the only one who has already participated in such a meeting, the others agree.

They start with a quick check-in where everybody can share how they feel at the moment and if there are any distractions from being fully present in the meeting. Catherine knows that this is a good way to have people 'land' in a meeting. Even if they don't share anything special, it helps participants to transition from a previous meeting or what they were doing before.

Then she asks Frank to share the driver statement they have prepared.

Frank begins to read. "In the last three promotion e-mails, the customer service number was not the right one. This leads to customers dialing the wrong number, being put on hold and yelling at customer service agents because they are frustrated from the long wait. We need better alignment between the marketing department and the customer service department to have satisfied customers and increase the NPS (Net Promoter Score)."
All four of them agree on the driver statement. Then Catherine asks Frank to read his proposal.

Frank reads: "The proposal is to have a customer service agent make a detailed list where products and customer service telephone numbers are matched. The marketing department then uses this list as a reference when creating e-mails."

Since nobody has any questions about the proposal, they go over to consent decision making. Because there are no objections, the proposal is accepted.

Considering there are no other topics scheduled, Catherine does a check-out. All four of them share how they feel now. The three others share that they are surprised how fast it went and how much energy they have left. Catherine nods and smiles. This is the usual effect of Compassionate Problem Solving.

Solving Personal Tension: The ABCs of De-stressing

There are many methods, techniques, and tools to solve personal tension, but one that I have found very useful is The ABCs of De-stressing technique by Marina Riemslagh.

Marina is the creator of the Live the Connection method. The ABCs of De-stressing is one of the techniques that are part of this method.

The real cause of stress

Marina has done extensive research into the field of stress. She provides a detailed description in her book *Stop Stress, Create Your Life. How to Resolve the Effects of Stress*. In this section, I present some of her key findings.

A real eye-opener for me was that all stress is related to a loss of control in one way or another.

Loss of control happens during a minor or major traumatic experience. The classic example is an accident. But it's much more. Every time you are startled or have moments of not knowing what is going to happen, you have to endure moments of loss of control. For example, when someone out of the blue started yelling at you when you were a child or when you were publicly humiliated as an adult.

When loss of control happens, we experience a (mini) blackout. At that moment, due to cortisol, the sensory signals are not clustered as a memory but attached to the amygdala in a fragmented way. In other words, loss of control is experienced as a traumatic event and coded by the brain as alarm emotions.

From now on, the amygdala will give an alarm trigger every time it perceives at least three of these sensory signals. Physically, this means a signal to the adrenal glands, which immediately provide the body with stress hormones (adrenaline and cortisol). The result is that your heart rate will go up, breathing becomes faster and shallower, blood pressure rises, digestion comes to a halt, and blood flows to the muscles in your limbs. The body prepares to fight, flight or freeze.

Fight, flight or freeze response

You probably have heard about the fight, flight or freeze response. But do you know what's behind each of these stress responses? Are you aware of the ways each stress response shows itself?

It's only when we start recognizing stress in ourselves and others that we can take action to solve it. So, let's look at a short summary based on the explanation in Marina Riemslagh's book.

Fight response

The underlying motive for a fight response is considering someone else as the cause of our stress. For people with this response, it's hard to see that the problem is internal (their own unconscious triggers).

These are some ways the fight response occurs:

- Showing superiority in a non-verbal way or passive-aggressiveness: literally taking up space (putting your stuff everywhere, so there is less room for others) or talking the whole time (leaving no room for others to contribute).
- Verbal domination: debating to convince others or to win, yelling, swearing, and demoralizing.
- Physical action: violence, slamming doors, and throwing plates against the wall.
- Proactively acting to damage 'the attacker': enforcing rules that others had not agreed to, controlling them, bringing up the past and gossiping.
- You are damaging yourself (when you see yourself as 'the other who is the cause of your stress'): self-mutilation, perfectionism and recklessly participating in dangerous sports.

Flight response

People with a flight response step out of contact. They indicate verbally and non-verbally that they are not present. They perceive the threat as too large to deal with.

These are some ways the flight response occurs:

- Wanting to get away: running away, getting out of the house/office, daydreaming, isolating, avoiding contact, and not coming back. And the extreme form: wanting to end your own life.
- Being absent: making yourself invisible, acting indifferently, denial, and using humor to change the topic.
- Being restless (because you want to get away, but you're physically not able): pacing around, being impatient or reacting in a panicky way.
- Seeking distractions and procrastination: doing something else then you are supposed to, worrying about other people or making a mess.
- Addictions: alcohol, sugar, porn, smoking, or gaming.

Freeze response

People with a freeze response have the most physical ailments. All original physical stress responses are fixated for a longer time. The consequence is that the adrenal glands, which increased the production of stress hormones get exhausted. Then more physical aches occur, immunity decreases, and diseases arise.

When people freeze, they have the impression they won't or can't do anything themselves. They are at the mercy of their body, other people, or society.

These are some ways the freeze response occurs:

- Feeling powerless or helpless: being silent, crying in a powerless way, and feeling hopeless.
- Feeling stuck: no emotion, feeling nothing at all, being unable to focus or decide, robotic or compulsive movements and being disoriented.
- Feeling tired and tense: aching shoulders, exhaustion, feeling weak or burned out.
- Internal struggle: appearing calm on the outside, but being nervous on the inside, having fears or panic attacks without knowing why and

experiencing internal chaos and drama. Usually, this is combined with a feeling of guilt about this internal struggle.

Let's see how Catherine applies this knowledge and The ABCs of De-stressing with Frank.

Gizmo Objects Inc.

Catherine is pleased with the results so far. Frank has transitioned from a negative to a positive vibe, one cause of frustration has been eliminated, and the relationship with the marketing department has improved.

She feels that Frank has much more potential than has come out so far. So, she starts paying more attention to him as a means of support. One of her observations is that he gets stressed when several people ask him questions at once. He tends to just listen without asking questions and then freezes.

The next time she notices this, she goes to Frank.

"Are you interested in learning another technique to remove stress?" she asks. "You already know the Compassion Technique when there is tension with someone else. Do you want to learn another technique to remove any other kind of stress?"

Frank quickly agrees. He feels safe and secure with Catherine. She treats him with respect and has already been very helpful. Both the Compassion Technique and Compassionate Problem Solving have helped him and the team. This has raised his trust in her. He is curious about what else she has to share.

"The technique I want to share with you is called The ABCs of De-stressing," Catherine says. "Let's go to a quiet room again, so we are not disturbed."

Catherine knows that it's not necessary to be in a quiet environment, but it helps. When it's the first time for someone, a quiet environment can feel more safe and secure.

"Just like with the Compassion Technique, you don't need to tell me what your stress is about. And you also don't need me or anyone else for The ABCs of De-stressing. When you have the instructions, you can do it on your own. But especially for the first time, it's more comfortable for someone to guide you. Is it OK that I first show you how to do it and then facilitate The ABCs of De-stressing for you?" Catherine asks.

Frank agrees, and Catherine demonstrates the ABCs of De-Stressing. When Frank indicates that he understands the procedure, she starts with the first of five steps. After only nine minutes, Frank finishes the last step.

When Catherine asks about his experience, Frank shares that he almost immediately felt something shift inside and that he feels more relaxed now. He thanks Catherine for her support and goes back to his desk. Catherine is delighted by Frank's openness and his willingness to grow.

The ABCs of De-stressing

The clue to de-stressing is to turn the process how stress is created around. It's about neutralizing the feeling of loss of control by clustering the sensory signals as a memory. As a result, they are not attached to the amygdala anymore, and the fight, flight or freeze response won't happen anymore.

The ABCs of De-stressing is another procedure that combines different short techniques to bring forward the best result. Some of these short techniques draw upon our rational capacities, while others draw upon our bodily senses. It's the combination that gets results.

The Steps of The ABCs of De-stressing

First we will go through the five steps of this procedure. An explanation of each step is presented in the next section.

For many people, it helps to follow the instructions in the free video where Marina Riemslagh takes you through the five steps. You can find it on her website: www.livetheconnection.com

Step A

Sit up straight, both feet flat on the ground, chin parallel to the floor, eyes focused down. Put your hand on your chest. Go to a place in your body where you experience love, that is the place your attention spontaneously goes to.

Say: *"My name is ... (your first name)."*

Step B

Experience the (stressful) situation by concentrating on it: feel it or think of it.

Step C

Say: *"It is in our highest good to create connections now."*
Say: *"This whole person now creates all connections by sitting in DNA string."*

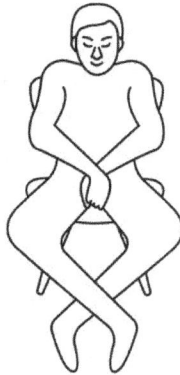

Step D

Sit in the strongest DNA string and close your eyes.
Concentrate on the (stressful) situation until the stress is gone.

After the stress is gone, your eyes spontaneously open.

Put your feet flat on the ground, next to one another and put your fingertips together for about 7 seconds.

Step E

Go back to the original (stressful) situation, and experience the difference. If you don't notice a difference, go on with D.

Look down and say: ***"In this situation, I remain totally connected."***

Put your hand on your chest. Go to a place in your body where you experience love and give thanks for the changes.

The ABCs of De-stressing Explained

As you can see, it is actually The ABCDE of De-stressing since there are five steps, but to keep it simple, Marina Riemslagh chose to call it The ABCs of De-stressing.

You might wonder what each step is about. The full explanation can be found in Marina's book: *Stop Stress, Create Your Life. How to Resolve the Effects of Stress.* You will discover that each word and gesture has a deep meaning behind it.

For now, I will share the topics that I deem the most important.

Step A: Make a connection with yourself

When keeping your head up and looking down, it's much easier to feel what is going on. Putting your hand on your chest and saying your name is necessary to make a true connection between the mind and body.

Step B: Decide which stress you want to release

Focusing on a stressful situation helps your system find the sensory signals that are attached to the amygdala. Those are the triggers you want to detach from the amygdala and combine to normal memory.

Step C: Connect and contract, involve the subconscious

By giving direct orders, the subconscious is involved. This is necessary to detach the triggers from the amygdala. First, you create safety for your inner system by saying, "It is in our highest good to create connections now." With the second phrase, "This whole person now creates all connections by sitting

127

in DNA string," you command your self-healing system to create connections between the triggers which make the load disappear.

As you can see in the visual, the term 'DNA string' points to the same position as the Whole Brain Position from the Compassion Technique. This position helps to rewire the different parts of the brain.

Step D: Making the connections

By sitting in the DNA string and thinking about or feeling the stressful situation, the triggers are detached from the amygdala and recombined as a normal memory. You can sit in the DNA string that feels the strongest to you: left ankle over right ankle or vice versa. The same applies for the arms.

The required time differs from person to person, and from situation of situation, but most people only need a few minutes. When this process is completed, your eyes open automatically. Just wait for it to happen while concentrating on the stressful situation.

Putting your fingertips together is a physical way of 'saving' the new memory like you would save a document on a computer.

Step E: Evaluating, noticing the difference and expressing gratitude

First, there is an evaluation. If you don't notice a difference, continue with step D. Usually this means that you opened your eyes too early and there is still some stress attached to this situation. Keep on focusing on that particular stressful situation. Stick to it and don't think of other stressful moments. You need one separate ABC for each stressful situation.

If you do notice a difference, the last sentence "In this situation, I remain totally connected." is the last confirmation that the triggers are now detached from the amygdala and won't lead to stress in this situation anymore.

Last but not least, there is an expression of gratitude. You are safe, and you can find this feeling of safety in yourself. You thank your body for the stress signals. Without them, you wouldn't have been able to turn the situation around. And you can be grateful for the fact that de-stressing has been possible.

Video

You can find the video where Marina Riemslagh takes you through the five steps and explains them on her website: www.livetheconnection.com

Note: Since the video of the technique is currently not that easy to locate on her website, you can find a detailed description of how to find it in the Training Center on the website of the Compassionate Leader.

Key Take-Aways

In the second step of the D.U.E.T. process, it's about first understanding the tension and then solving it.

Understanding the tension means putting it in one of three categories: interpersonal tension, practical/process tension, or personal tension.

The appropriate tool or technique to solve the tension is then applied:
- For interpersonal tension: The Compassion Technique.
- For practical or process tension: Compassionate Problem Solving.
- For personal tension: The ABCs of De-stressing.

One of the advantages of the Compassion Technique and The ABCs of De-stressing is that you or the person you facilitate don't have to share the details. This guarantees a feeling of safety and security.

An extra benefit of facilitating someone else going through the Compassion Technique or The ABCs of De-stressing is that it makes it easier to be present with someone else and hold the space for them. Since we are not used to being present with someone, it's easier to have a role like being a coach. However, the danger is that we want to provide solutions from our own experience. Then we get out of the 'being present' state. When facilitating someone else going through the Compassion Technique or The ABCs of De-stressing, you don't have to do anything but read the instructions. There is no expectation of solutions or advice. This is an easy way to hold the space for the other person.

This role of facilitator, where you only read the instructions and just be present, can be very liberating — especially if your job consists of making one decision after another day in day out.

Chapter 8

Embrace and Transform

the Root of the Tension

D.U.E.T. Process

1. Detect and face the tension		
2. Understand and solve the tension		
Interpersonal tension	Practical tension	Personal tension
Compassion Technique	Compassionate Problem Solving	The ABCs of De-stressing
3. Embrace and transform the root of the tension		
Compassion Quadrants	Compassionate Problem Solving	Inner Balance Technique
4. Take action		
Compassionate Communication	Apply the Proposal	Self Care

The third step of the D.U.E.T. process is about embracing and transforming the root of the tension.

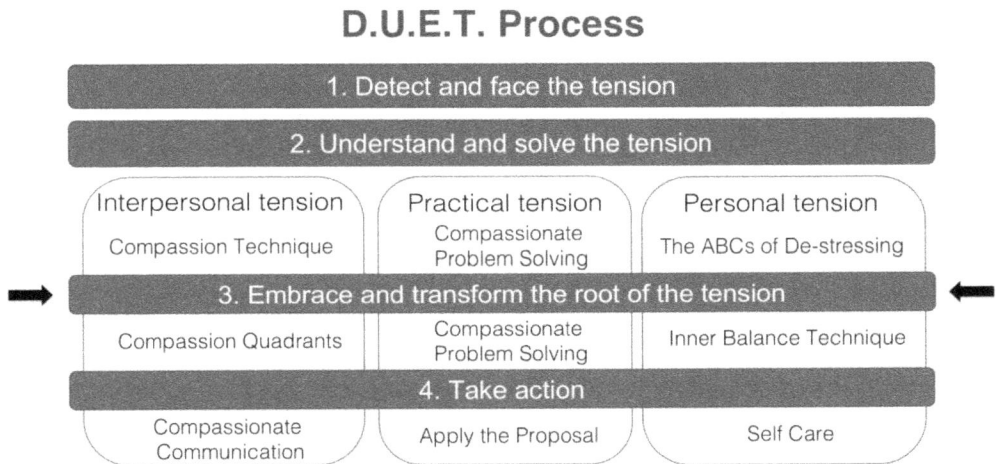

Sometimes there is no deeper root for the tension that was detected in Step 1, then this third step is not necessary. Or if one of the three techniques in Step 2 is enough, then this third step can be skipped.

In the cases where there is a deeper root, I have noticed that the cause of the tension is often situated in a different category than the tension that was detected in Step 1.

This doesn't surprise me. Since we often ignore tension until it has built up and mixed with other tensions, the first tension that is usually experienced is interpersonal tension. As explained in Chapter 2, when we (unconsciously) process tension by getting rid of it (by complaining, yelling, blaming) or suppressing it, this usually creates interpersonal tension.

When you and your team start to use the D.U.E.T. process more and more, this pattern changes. Then the tensions are detected before they can become interpersonal.

But, as I noticed, when individuals or teams are in the beginning phase of using the D.U.E.T. process, the focus is usually on first solving interpersonal tension.

Once that is done, the root of the tension can be embraced and transformed.

Embracing the root means being willing to face it and to be with it. This is similar to Step 1 (facing the tension), but since we are now a level deeper, it might be more challenging.

For example, it is often clear that after solving the interpersonal tension, there is a personal tension that is at the root. Personal tensions are usually linked to what we perceive as shadow sides. Our natural tendency is to ignore them or to avoid addressing them. The reason is that we fear they will be too painful to handle. In reality, the perceived potential pain is almost always much larger and exaggerated than the pain that is linked to the shadow side.

Since this perception is powerful, it's no surprise that many people have a hard time embracing the root of the initial tension. However, it is a necessary step. Otherwise, it will keep creating tensions in one way or another.

So, we first need to assess the situation:
- If the root of the tension is situated in another category, the techniques from Step 2 might be enough.
- If the root is in the same category and is not solved in Step 2, and it is about a practical or process tension, the Compassionate Problem Solving technique from the previous chapter can be used again.
- If the root is linked to a personal or interpersonal tension, exploring it can be a delicate task. That's why the facilitation of this process should be done by someone with the capacities of a Compassionate Leader. For the D.U.E.T. process, these capacities include postponing judgment, being centered, and having an open-mind towards what is hidden behind the tension and wants to be liberated or seen.

To transform the root of tension, these are the techniques that can be used:
- For interpersonal tension: Compassion Quadrants.
- For personal tension: Inner Balance Technique.

Let's see how Catherine from Gizmo Objects uses those tools.

Gizmo Objects Inc.

Customer service agent Frank and Marc, a member of the marketing team, are working on a project to redesign the pages of the customer service department on the website. This joint project of the customer service and marketing department is under the supervision of Catherine.

Although great ideas were formulated at the beginning of the project, nothing much has happened in the past month. Frank and Marc are having a hard time working together on the project.

Catherine notices this, and she decides to figure out what is happening. When she asks them in one-to-one conversations what is going on, Frank and Marc both express their frustration. Marc says that Frank is much too bureaucratic. In Marc's opinion, this attitude makes it hard to integrate new insights and technology that they discover along the way. Frank says that Marc is not consistent. In Frank's opinion, they will never be able to finish the project because Marc continuously wants to add new features and change the design.

Catherine thinks she sees what is going on here. But she knows that she might be wrong as well. That's why she takes a compassionate approach by first asking permission to offer her help and insights. Since she has been working for a while with them, she knows that the center of gravity of their vibes is positive. She feels that they don't need to use a tool like the Compassion Technique in this case. Instead, she is going to work with Compassion Quadrants and the Inner Balance Technique.

After Frank and Marc give her permission, she points out that they might have a conflict between two inner parts, not between them as a whole person. Before addressing those conflicting inner parts, she asks Frank and Marc if they can point out the areas where they get along. She explains that the easiest way to do this is to list a few positive traits of the other person. This helps to put the situation in perspective and brings more openness. Frank and Marc do this. They both feel that this takes the edge off the tension between them.

Catherine points out that the conflict might be about the excessive behavior of one inner part of Frank versus the excessive behavior of one inner part of Marc. She explains that it is behavior that probably is trying to protect an inner part. Usually, it is a positive quality that goes in overdrive and as a consequence shows negative behavior. She also adds that it is not about deliberately attacking the other person but about protecting oneself. This shift from focusing on the behavior to focusing on the quality brings more openness and compassion to the situation.

When they do the Compassion Quadrants exercise, they discover that Frank's bureaucratic behavior shows too much of his positive core quality *bringing structure*. In Marc's case, his inconsistent behavior shows too much of his positive core quality *flexibility*. This insight makes Frank and Marc open up even more to each other.

Catherine also knows that when people are triggered by each other's behavior, there is an imbalance between their *own* inner parts. She asks Frank if he could use more flexibility and asks Marc if he could use more structure. They both agree.

"Can you see that the other person is a trigger of something from the past," asks Catherine, "and not the cause of your current feeling of discomfort? And can you see that the other person offers a pointer to a part of you that was invisible to you?"

Frank and Marc agree. Now they can look at each other from another perspective. Not only can they see the positive quality behind the behavior that frustrated each of them, but they consider this situation as a gift. They have discovered a primary self in themselves that is too present and a disowned self that is not present enough or not present at all.

Marc and Frank are grateful for these insights and for Catherine's facilitation of the process. Frank chooses to take a 15-minute break to apply the 'short' version of the Inner Balance Technique to integrate the primary and disowned self. Marc admits that they have uncovered a recurring theme in his life. He wants to investigate its roots deeper and makes an appointment with a coach to use the insights from this short session with Catherine as input for a 'normal' Inner Balance Technique session.

Catherine is pleased with the outcome. She is also not surprised anymore how fast this happens. In the beginning, when she learned all the techniques from the D.U.E.T. process, the sessions she facilitated needed more time and attention. But she knows that that is part of how learning something new works. It always takes some time to master a technique or tool.

She also admits that applying the different techniques with herself and others led to understanding the depths of them, not just theoretical knowledge. One of the insights she is grateful for relates to conflict: she now understands that the positive quality behind the other person's negative behavior is linked to her own disowned self. This was hard to admit for her as long as she kept focusing on the *behavior* of the other person. It was only by seeing that this behavior protects a positive quality, that she could be more open to the other person. And then to her own disowned self.

Finding the Root of Interpersonal Tension: Compassion Quadrants

When there is tension between people, the first step would be to apply the Compassion Technique. This helps to relax and become more open and even compassionate towards the other person. The result is that it becomes easier to explore the cause or root of the tension. When you are still upset or sad or feel powerless, then it's difficult to be open to explore the root. In the moments when you don't feel those heavy emotions, you don't need the Compassion Technique. You can start immediately with the Compassion Quadrants.

The Compassion Quadrants are based on the Core Quadrants by Daniel Ofman. For a deeper understanding of his inspiring work, you can read his books *Building Commitment and Enthusiasm in Organizations* and *Fancy Meeting Me Here*.

Core Quadrants

This is an example of what the Core Quadrants (or Core Qualities) model looks like:

Core Quality

Core Quality	Too much of this positive aspect →	**Pitfall**
Patience		Passivity
↑ Positive opposite		Positive opposite ↓
Pushiness	← Too much of this positive aspect	Pro-activity
Allergy		**Challenge**

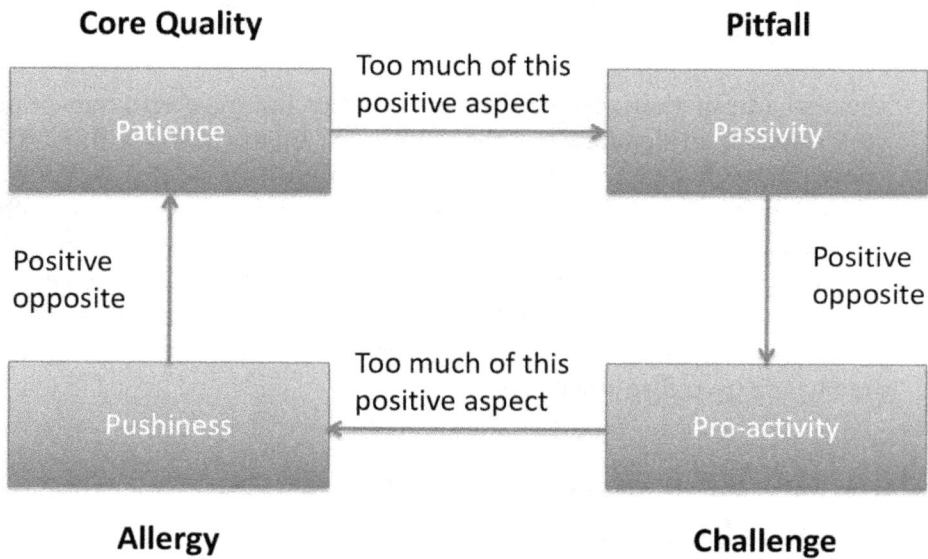

How does it work?

Let's use the picture above as an example; starting top left and rotating clock-wise.

- The Core Quality of this person is Patience. This is a positive quality.
- Too much of this Core Quality is Passivity. This is the Pitfall for this person.
- The positive opposite of the Pitfall is Pro-activity. This is this person's Challenge. This is a positive quality.
- Too much of this Challenge is Pushiness. That is this person's Allergy.
- The positive opposite of the Allergy is Patience. And we are back at the Core Quality.

Here is a list with more details to provide you with a better understanding of what the quadrants entail.

- Core quality: positive quality
  - What I think is normal (about me)
  - What others appreciate about me
  - What I encourage in others
  - What I expect or demand from others

- Pitfall: exaggeration of a positive quality, so it becomes negative
    o What others blame me for
    o What I am willing to forgive in others
    o What I justify about myself
- Challenge: positive quality, that is asking to be balanced in our life (opposite of Core Quality)
    o What I admire in others
    o What I lack in myself
    o What others wish for me
- Allergy: exaggeration of a positive quality, so it becomes negative
    o What I despise in others
    o What I would hate in myself
    o What I have to tolerate in others (but hardly can)

What does it mean in practice?

Core Quality: This is a strength, something that comes naturally to you, but not to others. They think it's amazing that you have this talent, but most of the time you think it's no big deal. It comes naturally to you. At the same time, many people feel that they're not worth much or don't have much to contribute. In other words, often there is a blind spot here: one of your core qualities that you are not aware of. So, the goal is to see and acknowledge your qualities (again).

Pitfall: This is too much of a Core Quality. This is what people blame you for. The consequence is that since we feel attacked on the Pitfall, we don't look at the Core Quality either.

Challenge: This is a positive quality that can use more attention. It's something to balance in your life. It's something that gives you more joy. However, most of the time, we don't see it because the Allergy blocks the path towards it.

Allergy: This is too much of the Challenge. It is the 'negative' opposite of a Core Quality. This is what pushes your buttons. Since it can make you even furious, it blocks seeing the positive quality of the Challenge.

Double Quadrants

A double quadrant can be used to understand another person better. It starts with your own quadrant, and then you add another quadrant starting from one of the four boxes.

This is an example of a double quadrant:

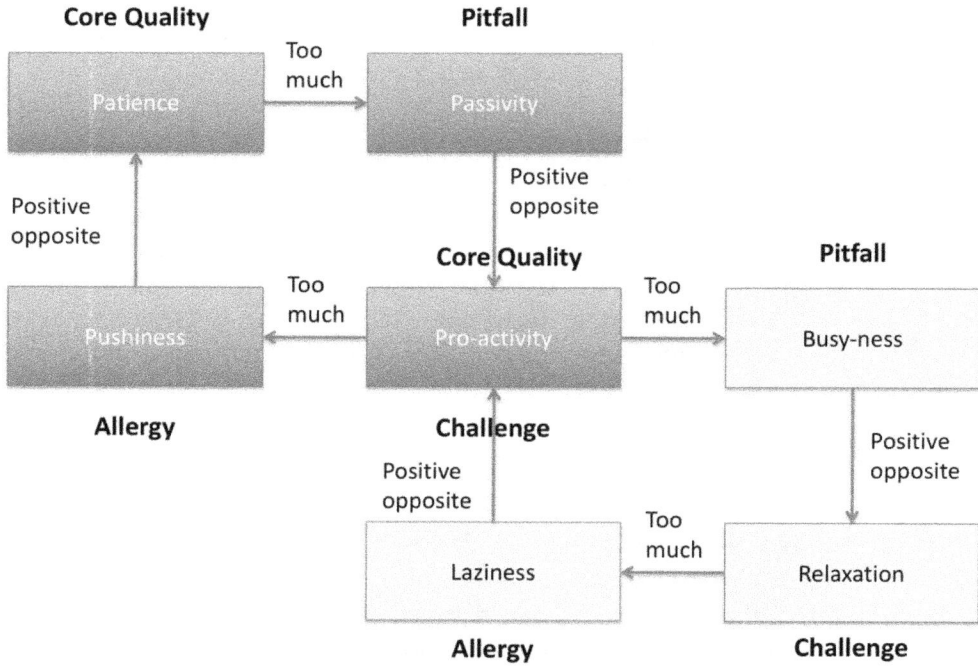

In this case, we use the Challenge to start a double quadrant. So, we start from our own Challenge. This is the other person's Core Quality. Then we can make a quadrant for them. This could be exactly the same as our quadrant, but usually, the accents are a bit different.

In this case, we might perceive the other person in our quadrant as being pushy. This is our Allergy, which is too much about being proactive. However, when we focus on the other person, the Pitfall of the Core Quality of Proactivity might be rather Busy-ness. For this person, the Pitfall is being busy all the time, not taking time to Relax. This is his Challenge. However, since he is Allergic to Laziness, the chances are high that he has a hard time relaxing.

For this example, we started with our Challenge as the other person's Core Quality. You can also start from the other boxes: our Pitfall as the other person's Allergy, our Core Quality as the other person's Challenge, and our Allergy as the other person's Pitfall.

Compassion Quadrants

Compassion Quadrants are very similar to Core Quadrants, but there are a few important distinctions:

- In Compassion Quadrants, we work with inner parts. The Core Quality is a positive quality of a primary part, and the Challenge is a positive quality of a disowned part.
- The goal is to embrace and transform the root of the tension that was felt in interaction with another person.
- We can use the insights from the Compassion Quadrants as input for the Inner Balance Technique to transform the root of personal tension as well.

The Compassion Quadrants model can help to discover one of your Core Qualities (positive quality of a primary self) and one of your own Challenges (positive quality of a disowned self). You will also be less judging and more compassionate towards other people because you will understand from which Core Quality or Challenge their behavior originates.

The interesting thing about this model is that you can start using it from every quadrant. Since the focus of this technique in the D.U.E.T. process is to transform the root of interpersonal tension, the easiest entrances are what you are experiencing:

- Allergy: your blames or complaints about another person.
- Pitfall: someone else's blames or complaints about you.

Starting from the Allergy or Pitfall, you can easily discover primary and disowned selves and their positive qualities.

It also helps in your interactions with other people.

Every time you hear yourself judge someone (you blame or complain because you are 'allergic' to their behavior), stop yourself and wonder: "Which positive quality am I focused on? Which Challenge is this person pointing me towards? Which of my disowned inner parts need attention?" The answer you receive is a quality you can develop in yourself. It's a quality that can help you become more balanced and more centered. You can also ask yourself: "What is the positive opposite of this behavior that I'm allergic to? To which Core Quality of one of my own inner parts is this person pointing me?"

You can also use a similar way of reframing the situation when someone judges you. When they blame or complain about you, don't get defensive. Discover what Core Quality is too much on the forefront (which shows as your Pitfall). When you hear someone blame you, think about which positive quality is too present, which primary self is too dominant. This way, you can discover a Core Quality, something you are good at.

The blaming person might provide another insight as well. They may point you to a Challenge: the positive opposite of the blame. This is a positive quality of a disowned self.

Since many times our Core Qualities or primary selves are blind spots to us and the Challenges or disowned selves are unknown, the Compassion Quadrants model offers great insights by starting from a Pitfall or Allergy.

Besides getting more insight in yourself, you may get a totally different perspective on this person who is blaming you or to whom you are allergic. Instead of pushing him away, you can thank him for his contribution in discovering more about yourself. Depending on the situation and the kind of relationship you have, you can say it loud or just do it in your mind. Whatever you choose, you will feel your compassion level increase.

Insights and dynamics

From this short introduction, it is already clear that (Double) Compassion Quadrants offer some very good insights into our situation and our relationship with the other person.

Let's use them to look a bit deeper into human behavior and how we can resolve conflicts and confusion.

Compassion Quadrants help to separate the negative behavior from positive qualities. Human beings are triggered by other people's behavior, resulting in Allergies and Pitfalls. What usually happens is that we get stuck on the behavior level. We use words like "He is pushy" or "She is lazy".

Thanks to the Compassion Quadrants, we now know that it works differently. Someone might behave pushily, but that's just too much of the positive quality of Pro-activity. Someone might behave lazily, but that's just too much of Relaxation.

In other words, the Compassion Quadrants model helps to detect the deeper positive qualities and intentions below behavior that might be perceived as negative on the surface.

We have also learned that irritations and conflicts are about the behavior of inner selves. This means that we cannot only rephrase the sentence "She is lazy" to "She behaves lazily" (which already feels different, because it addresses the behavior instead of someone's identity), but to "There is a part in her that seems to be behaving lazily."

From my own experience, the rephrasing of this sentence changes a lot. When I say this to myself about another person, it becomes easier to deal with the situation. When the sentence is, "She is lazy," it feels like nothing can be done about the situation. When I don't like lazy people, my strategy is to avoid this person. When the sentence is, "There is a part in her that seems to be behaving lazily," the situation changes completely. I can see that there are many other parts in the other person than just the one that is currently behaving in a negative way. I can also be more compassionate toward the lazy part. And because of the Compassion Quadrants, I can see that it's too much of one of her Core Qualities (Relaxation) and something that I don't give enough attention to myself. This turns the situation around. Now I can see her in a positive light. I can be grateful for the discovery of one of my disowned selves.

A second insight is that the invitation of the Core Quadrants model is to connect the Core Quality and the Challenge. When we can do this, we can live a more balanced and harmonious life.

We can use the literal words from the Core Quadrants model to describe this balanced state. For example, Patient Pro-activity, Proactive Patience, Relaxed Pro-activity, or Pro-active Relaxation.

This combined phrase might be a little weird at first, but most people not only feel the balance when it is worded like this but also both the peace and power it contains.

I emphasize this because many busy people are told that they need to relax. However, this might feel to them that they are judged and condemned by others for being proactive. It feels like relaxation is sacred, and being proactive is of the devil. But since Pro-activity is a very important quality to them, they won't give it up. On the contrary, they might resist Relaxation even more.

However, like the Core Quadrants model shows, it's not about one or the other, it's about combining them. It is about balancing the Core Quality and the Challenge. That way, both positive qualities can reinforce and support each other.

The Compassion Quadrants teach us that this balance includes a primary self on the one hand and a disowned self on the other. Once we have discovered them, we can use the Inner Balance Technique (see the next section in this chapter) to harmonize them. In that way, the primary and disowned self work together. The result is that you can reach your goals faster and with less effort.

A third insight is related to the dynamics of Pitfall and Allergy.

While combining the Core Quality and the Challenge leads to balance, the dynamics of the Pitfall and the Allergy keep the conflict between people going (which means continuing or increasing the interpersonal tension) or creating inner stress (personal tension).

Let's use the example again where Pushiness is the Allergy and Passivity is the Pitfall. Let's assume that they are other qualities and excesses of customer service agent Frank and marketing team member Marc.

This is how this shows in reality.

1. Frank is frustrated because of Marc's pushy behavior. Since Frank doesn't want to be pushy at all (because his Core Quality is Patience), he behaves passively to slow down the pushy behavior of Marc (Frank's Passivity is his Pitfall, which is too much of his Core Quality Patience).
2. Marc is frustrated because of Frank's passive behavior. Since Marc doesn't want to be passive (because his Core Quality is Pro-activity), he behaves in a pushy way to get the passive behavior of Marc in motion (Marc's Pushiness is his Pitfall, which is too much of his Core Quality Proactivity).
3. This continues for a while, creating a negative spiral downwards.
4. What could happen at some point in time is that Frank becomes so angry about Marc's behavior on the one hand, and feels so powerless to change anything about the situation on the other, that he becomes pushy as well. As a last resort, he jumps from his Pitfall to his Allergy. Usually this doesn't solve much about the tense situation with Marc. On the contrary, this aggravates the situation with Marc ànd causes

inner tension within Frank. Now Frank feels an inner struggle on top of the conflict with Marc: he is behaving in a pushy way, something that he condemns. So, he now criticizes himself, creating even more inner personal tension. Since he doesn't want to feel this way, he projects his inner struggle to Marc and blames him for being the cause of the conflict.

In step 4, Frank criticizes himself. This boils down to his primary self condemning his disowned self, pushing his disowned self, together with its positive qualities, even further away. As a result, Frank's inner tension increases.

In this example, you recognize four of the 'strategies of the ego': judging, projection, victimhood, and self-criticism. As you can see, The Compassion Quadrants model is an excellent tool to avoid getting carried away by those strategies and to transform the root of tensions.

How to apply the Compassion Quadrants

Since our main focus in this part of the D.U.E.T. process is to embrace and transform the root of interpersonal tension, understanding why the other person's behavior is bothering you can be used as an entry point.

Part 1: Create the Compassion Quadrant

These are the steps:

- Draw the four quadrants with four empty boxes (see visual below).
- Start with filling out the Allergy. This is the behavior of the other person that is bothering you. For example: pushiness.
- Then go up: fill out the positive opposite of the Allergy in the Core Quality box. For example: patience.
- Then go right: describe your behavior that is too much of the Core Quality. This is your Pitfall. For example: passivity.
- Then go down: fill out the positive opposite of the Pitfall in the Challenge box for example: proactivity.
- Then go left: check if the Allergy is too much of the Challenge. If that is not the case, try to refine the words you put in each box.

Important: It is more essential to feel what the exercise is doing with you than to have the exact words in each box.

Core Quality   **Pitfall**

Too much of this
positive aspect

Positive
opposite   Positive
opposite

Too much of this
positive aspect

Allergy   **Challenge**

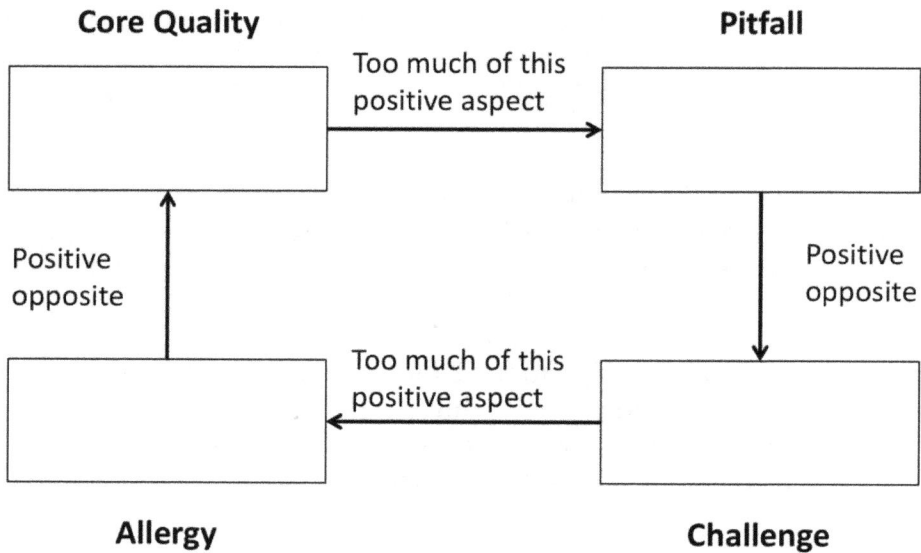

These are a few examples of Core Quadrants:

Core Quality	Pitfall	Challenge	Allergy
Flexibility	Chaos	Organization	Rigidity
Courage	Recklessness	Thoughtfulness	Doubtfulness
Profiling	Arrogance	Modesty	Invisibility
Helpfulness	Interference	Autonomy	Indifference

You can find more examples in the Training Center on the website.

Part 2: Create the Double Compassion Quadrant

If you want to understand the other person better, you can create a Double Compassion Quadrant. You don't have to do this step. You can also just create the Compassion Quadrant for yourself and then go to part 3 of the exercise.

However, a double Compassion Quadrant can provide you with lots of insights about the other person.

You can start from any quadrant. However, most people find it useful to start from their own Challenge and use that as the other person's Core Quality.

Part 3: Insights and Actions

After creating the Compassion Quadrant, I invite you to look at it and to consider this:

- Understand that your own Pitfall is just too much of a positive quality. When other people react negatively, consider this a reminder to slow down and go back to the essence of the Core Quality.
- Understand that your Allergy is too much of a positive quality that needs more space in your life. The more you fight this Allergy, the more you block access to the positive quality of your disowned self. As a consequence, your primary self goes in overdrive to protect you. Then a Core Quality becomes a Pitfall. This gives tension with other people and tension in yourself.
- Be grateful for the other person helping you discover one of your own Core Qualities: the positive quality of a primary self.
- Be grateful for the other person helping you to discover one of your Challenges: the positive quality of a disowned self.

By taking a few minutes to go through these sentences, you will feel the compassion increase for you and the other person.

If you have created a Double Compassion Quadrant, look at it and then go through these invitations:

- Notice how the Pitfall of the other person is just too much of a positive quality. See if you can look through the negative behavior and find the other person's Core Quality behind the Pitfall.
- Observe how their Allergy keeps them from benefiting from the positive quality of a Challenge.
- Realize that their behavior is not who they are, but that it's just one of their inner selves pushing too hard.
- Recognize that both of you feel the tensions of inner selves and that you offer pointers to one another in the form of an Allergy and a Pitfall.
- See if you can accept this shared humaneness.

Again, if you take the time, you will feel an increase in compassion for the other person and yourself.

The increase in compassion usually creates more openness and willingness to take a new action. Decide which one is right for you:

- Applying the Inner Balance Technique (see below) to balance a Core Quality and a Challenge, to balance a primary and a disowned self.
- Using these insights to start a new conversation with the other person. You can use the tips regarding Compassionate Communication (see chapter 9) for even better results.
- Doing nothing yet, but come back to the (Double) Compassion Quadrant a few times in the next couple of days to let the insight in the dynamics between you and the other person and between your primary and disowned self sink in a bit deeper. Use these insights to change your behavior or react differently to other people's behavior. However, without balancing the inner selves, that will be a lot harder.

Embracing and Transforming the Root of Personal Tensions: The Inner Balance Technique

We have all set goals (like reaching a sales target, learning a language or losing weight) that we couldn't achieve. It's like one foot presses the gas pedal and the other foot pushes the brake at the same time. It feels like there is some kind of sabotage mechanism that prevents us from reaching that goal.

Actually, it's about two parts in us that are not balanced.

The Inner Balance Technique is a tool that helps to balance those two parts so the sabotage mechanism becomes a supporting mechanism instead. Not only can you reach your goal, but achieving the result will require less effort.

If you have created a Compassion Quadrant or detected your primary and disowned selves in another way, you have taken the first step.

The next step is to balance them so they can work together from their positive qualities (Core Quality and Challenge) instead of fighting each other from their excesses (Pitfall or Allergy).

The short version of the Inner Balance Technique is to be aware of the two inner selves and then apply The ABCs of De-stressing (see chapter 7). Focus in step 2 on the two inner parts.

An alternative to the ABCs of De-stressing is the Compassion Technique. Then the focus is not on another person, but on the *disowned self*. If necessary, the Compassion Technique is applied one more time with the focus on the *primary inner self* as well.

For some people, applying the ABCs of De-stressing or the Compassion Technique to the two inner parts is enough. For other people, it's not. Then the 'normal' Inner Balance Technique can be done with a certified coach.

The reason for sharing this short version is to provide you with a technique you can do on your own, whenever you need it. In cases where the emotional burden is not so heavy, the short version of the Inner Balance Technique is a good tool.

However, many people have a hard time doing this on their own. When there's a tension with another person, it's not easy to avoid going into defensive mode, detect underlying behavior, or find the primary or disowned selves. In those cases, the 'normal' version of the Inner Balance Technique is needed. This is a one-to-one session with a certified coach.

Besides the fact that there is the insightful help and compassionate presence of a coach who offers a safe space, an Inner Balance Technique session includes these ingredients:

- Help to get centered. If necessary, by using the Compassion Technique, the ABCs of De-stressing or another tool.
- Detecting the opposite inner self. If necessary, by using Compassion Quadrants or another tool.
- Deep inquiry in the motives, origins of the behavior and needs of each inner self. If necessary, by using extra tools like Voice Dialogue or Systemic Work/Constellations.
- Facilitated Compassionate Communication between the two selves.
- Profound balancing of the two selves.

Blind spots and inner selves are often not an easy issue, but detecting and balancing them can give your life an enormous boost. A certified coach with a compassionate attitude offers both the outside view and a safe and stimulating environment that can be crucial for a breakthrough.

Key Take-Aways

If there is a deeper root or cause, then the third step of the D.U.E.T. process is needed.

In the third step, the focus is on finding, embracing, and transforming the root of the tension.

Tools and techniques that are used in this step are:
- For interpersonal tension: Compassion Quadrants;
- For practical or process tension: Compassionate Problem Solving;
- For personal tension: The Inner Balance Technique.

The Compassion Quadrants model allows detecting the positive qualities behind negative behavior. This helps to find the root of conflicts between people and become more compassionate towards them. It also reveals which primary selves are too dominant and which disowned selves are hiding. The consequence is more compassion for yourself.

The Inner Balance Technique offers a method to balance primary and disowned selves. There is a 'short' version that individuals can do by themselves or a 'normal' version, which is facilitated by a certified coach. As a result, the foot is lifted from the brake, and sabotage mechanisms are transformed into support mechanisms.

Chapter 9

Take Action

D.U.E.T. Process

1. Detect and face the tension		
2. Understand and solve the tension		
Interpersonal tension	Practical tension	Personal tension
Compassion Technique	Compassionate Problem Solving	The ABCs of De-stressing
3. Embrace and transform the root of the tension		
Compassion Quadrants	Compassionate Problem Solving	Inner Balance Technique
4. Take action		
Compassionate Communication	Apply the Proposal	Self Care

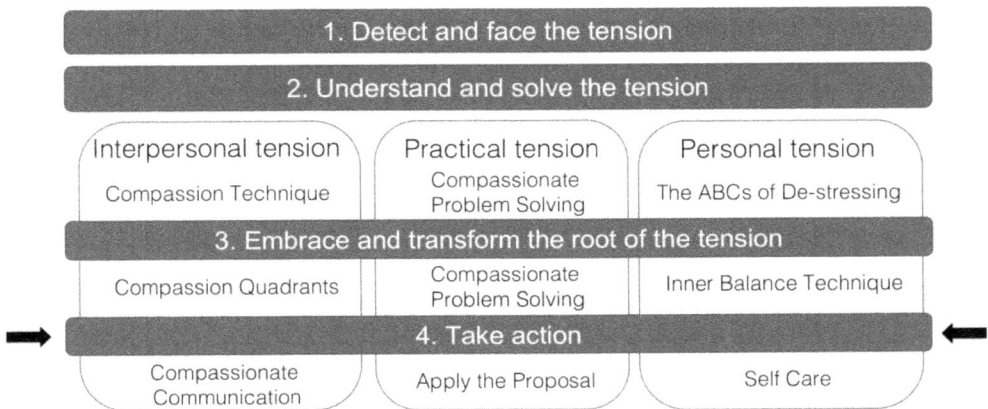

The fourth step of the D.U.E.T. process is about taking action.

Depending on the type of tension you are dealing with, there are several ways to take action.

When the tension is a **practical** one, applying the proposal that was formulated via the Compassionate Problem Solving Technique is usually sufficient.

For example:
- Extra code in the order and shipping software to automatically alert the warehouse that goods need to be packaged.
- Scanners and scanning software to solve the manual input problem.
- Implementation of a structured meeting approach.

In the case of Gizmo Objects Inc., the action was creating a list where the products and telephone numbers of the customer service department are matched.

When the tension is of a **personal or interpersonal** nature, understanding the root is sometimes enough to start a natural transformation process. However, often, other or extra steps might be necessary.

These are the most common ones:
- Start a conversation using Compassionate Communication.
- Focus on self-care.

Important note: Compassionate Communication can be used at any moment. It is not necessary to first go through steps 2 (understand and solve the tension) and 3 (embrace and transform the root of the tension) of the D.U.E.T. process before you can apply Compassionate Communication. In other words, when there is not enough time and space, you can skip steps 2 and 3 and immediately apply Compassionate Communication. However, as you will read below, steps 2 and 3 are very useful when preparing for a difficult conversation.

Compassionate Communication

When tension occurs at the interpersonal level, you might want to share your own insights or the one you got from working with the Compassion Quadrants with the other person. Or approach them to talk about a need or a concern.

However, since this is probably not the first time that you experienced tension with this person, the chances are high that you already attempted to have a conversation in the past, but to no avail. It is only normal that you are not inclined to try it again without a new approach or support.

Enter Compassionate Communication.

This method of communication can be used in any situation (it doesn't even have to be a situation where you experience tension). It's about starting any conversation from a compassionate attitude. You can use it both for listening and speaking. You can use it when you are *listening* to the other person to detect what they need or how you can support them. And you can use it when you are *voicing* your own need or formulating a request.

Compassionate Communication is focused on getting a result and improving the relationship at the same time. Usually, the focus of a conversation is only on getting a result (without taking the relationship into account and as a result damaging it in one way or another) or improving the relationship (without getting a result or clarity which often leads to misunderstandings or frustration afterward).

Compassionate Communication is especially useful in situations when people find it difficult to express their needs or concerns. They can have a hard time expressing themselves (speaking) or understanding someone else (listening). In both situations, Compassionate Communication can be used.

Compassionate Communication consists of four aspects. It is not necessary to take all four into account at once. However, the more aspects you use, the more compassionate your communication will be. However, using one or two aspects might already make a big difference compared with the past.

The four aspects are:
1. Attitude
2. Openness and Clarity
3. Words
4. Structure

Once you have learned about them, I invite you to start with the aspect that is the easiest for you and then add more.

Attitude

The foundation of Compassionate Communication is a compassionate attitude.

This starts with considering the other person as equal, not smaller nor larger, not a victim nor a savior.

Behavior-wise an essential element is to first ask for permission. This is not only compassionate behavior, but it also helps the other person to be in the conversation with you instead of in their head. It helps them to be more present.

Sentences you can use:
- "Can I ask you something?"
- "I hear you are worried about something. I might have a suggestion. Do you want to hear it?"
- "Can I ask you for some advice?"

Showing a compassionate attitude and asking for permission is applicable in any situation.

Also, don't openly blame another person, even when it's their fault. It puts them in a defensive position where it's hard to get a solution. That's why we like to work with Compassionate Problem Solving for practical tensions since there is no blaming involved.

For situations where people are having a hard time expressing or finding the essence of the situation, I have some extra tips.

When people find it difficult to voice their needs or concerns, often there are emotions involved like frustration, anger, or sadness. Or there is a withdrawal due to a feeling of hopelessness or powerlessness.

When there are emotions involved, it usually translates into some kind of negative behavior. This behavior is what puts others in a defensive mode.

The first key to turn this situation around is determining if it's a primary or disowned self that is expressing itself. The primary self usually acts to protect. The disowned self usually acts to be seen. When there is a withdrawal, the primary or disowned self perceives the situation as too difficult to act. Then it experiences hopelessness or powerlessness.

The second key is noticing that all the other selves of this person are NOT acting out. In other words, it is just a small part of the person that is showing negative behavior. Realizing this – whether or not having consciously done the exercise of pointing out the positive qualities of the other-selves of this person – helps to put the situation into another perspective.

The third key is understanding that when a primary or disowned self is acting out, it's not balanced with the other self. You can experience this as something negative, but you could also look at it from a positive angle. It means that there is room for growth and an opportunity to have things go smoother in life. When inner parts are not balanced, they consume a lot of – mental – energy to protect (primary self) or to ask for attention (disowned self). When they are balanced, they not only consume less energy, but they also reinforce each other.

This third key is a very important insight when we want to grow further as a person and support our team members to grow as well. For teams that want to be in the inspiring vibe and want to be truly self-managing, this is a crucial step to take.

Without this step, people will stay in a positive vibe. This is also a very nice vibe to be in (and usually higher than most people are in today), it just depends on the ambitions and challenges of your team. In today's VUCA (Volatile, Uncertain, Complex, Ambiguous) world, there are teams or companies that need to tackle complex and global issues. They can't afford to have primary or disowned selves sabotage ideas or the decision-making process.

Or to look at it from a more positive side: when there is less friction because of primary or disowned selves acting out, there is much more room for ideas and solutions to emerge and be pursued. Daily work goes smoother, and problems are solved faster. It becomes much easier to reach goals and go beyond them.

As a summary, the first aspect for Compassionate Communication is the **attitude** which includes:
- Consider the other person equal.
- Ask for permission first.
- When the other person is showing negative behavior or when you feel resistance or tension about the other person, keep this in mind:
    - It is just a primary or disowned self that is playing out.
    - All their other selves are NOT showing negative behavior.
    - There is an imbalance between a primary and disowned self.

Openness and clarity

The second aspect of a successful conversation is openness and clarity.

If you know you are going to have a conversation with someone else that might be difficult because of interpersonal tensions, it might be good to prepare for it. On the one hand, being open and clear might help to alleviate the conversation becoming difficult. On the other hand, being open and clear helps to keep the conversation focused. Then the chance decreases that extra tensions are created or that the vibe goes down.

One way of preparing is applying the Compassion Technique. This usually brings more peace and openness towards the other person.

A second way of preparing yourself for the conversation is to create a (Double) Compassion Quadrant. This will help to see upfront where the other person and yourself might get into a negative spiral: when they are behaving in a way a part of you is Allergic to, you normally would (unconsciously) go into the Pitfall of that inner self.

By preparing upfront, you might be aware of the dynamics and avoid being overwhelmed by them. This helps to stay focused on one of your own Core Qualities as well as on one from the other person (= your Challenge). It will also remind you that if there is a tension between the two of you, it is just between one inner self of you and one inner self of the other person. All the other inner selves are not in conflict and are probably willing to make the best out of the situation.

When it's about something practical, a third way of preparing is to create a statement like in Compassionate Problem Solving. This includes the bigger picture, avoids blaming others, and brings clarity. The result is that chances are higher that the other person doesn't move into a defensive position and that they are more open to finding a solution that works for everybody.

You can also use the Compassion Technique and Compassion Quadrants *after* the conversation.

For example, the Compassion Technique can be used when you felt disadvantaged by the other person and were not able to voice it. Then you can use the Compassion Technique to calm down and create an openness for the next conversation with this person.

Compassion Quadrants can be used if you were triggered by the other person and ended up in an Allergy or Pitfall. You can use the situation to discover one of your Core Qualities or a Challenge or to find a primary and disowned self that need balance. You can also create a Double Quadrant to understand the other person better and be more prepared for a next conversation.

Words

The third aspect of Compassionate Communication is about the literal words you use.

Many words are used daily that can create tension with other people without us being aware of it.

Those words include connotations of separation and struggle. Again, we are usually not aware of it. However, they do not help create good relationships or achieve goals.

My invitation is to become aware of the language you are using. By using less war-like language and more harmonious words, you will have less conflict with other people (less interpersonal tensions) and experience less personal tension as well.

What are some of the words to look out for?

All war-like words

War-like words include attack, defense, destroy, annihilate, offense, retreat, assault, protect, aggressive, fortify, guard, shield, trenches, weapons or ammunition.

This kind of language is especially used in sports and corporate environments:
- Corporate environments:
  o "We have to arm ourselves for the next quarter."
  o "We have to defend our market share."
  o "Let's pull the trigger on this issue."
  o "We have to attack a specific target group."
- Sports:
  o Most sports talk about offense and defense. There are also many *offensive* and *defensive* strategies in any sports.
  o "We have them by the throat."
  o "That shot was the final blow for the team. It felt like an execution."
  o "We have to crush the enemy."

Pay attention to these words and how you use them. If you don't use these phrases, think about the ones you do use that could be considered war-like. Ask for help if your words and phrases are blind spots to you.

The word 'But'

Have you paid attention to what happens when you or someone else uses the word *but* in a sentence?

"I appreciated you doing the dishes yesterday, *but* how could you forget to use the vacuum cleaner? I put it right in front of the door."

Two things are happening in this specific sentence:

- The word *but* wipes out everything that precedes it. It's like a verbal eraser. People don't remember the words before *but* anymore. The word *but* is like a red flag: this is what you are doing wrong, and because of that reason I'm rejecting you or attacking you.
- If you read this sentence out loud, like if you were saying it to someone, can you notice how it builds up to the *but*? We are so trained in how people do this, that we are already anticipating the *but* coming when people seem to be praising us. In other words, we are already preparing for the rejection or attack. When we are already in a defensive mode, we are no longer listening to what the message or the intention is behind the message. We are only focused on our defense.

What can you do instead? A simple solution is to replace the word *but* with the word *and*. It might be difficult in the beginning because you also have to change the pace of your sentence. However, the more you consciously do this, the easier it will become.

The words 'Yes, but'

A variation on *but* is *yes, but*. It actually works the same way.

Both *but* and *yes, but* are signs that we are fighting to be right. The question many authors and coaches ask is, "Would you rather be right or happy?" Many people protest: "When I'm right, I'm right. I won't give it up." However, many times we're not fighting for what it's about, for the content. The *but*, or the *yes, but* are patterns of fighting for dominance. They are about a victim-persecutor pattern.

What you will see happening is that when you enter the conversation with a compassionate attitude, and openness and clarity, what is 'right' (whether it is your opinion or the other person's opinion) will be the outcome of the conversation. Or, something better will come up. In this way you won't only keep the relationship harmonious, but you'll also get better results.

Exaggerations

Exaggerations are words like ever, never, always.

When you use words like these, people will go in defensive mode. They will perceive those words as not reflecting the truth, but rather as an attack.

Example: when you are frustrated that you had to take the garbage cans out again instead of your partner (and it's their chore), the conversation usually goes like this:

- You: "You *never* take the garbage out."
- Your partner: "*Never*? I did it three weeks ago."
- You: "And before? I *always* have to do your chores."
- Your partner: "The only thing you *always* do is exaggerate."

As a result, the problem is not solved, and a new interpersonal tension is created.

The words 'should, ought, must, need.'

These are words to pay attention to, especially in your self-talk. I think it's obvious when you tell someone, "You *must* do the dishes," that they will go into defensive mode. For me, words like *should, ought, must* and *need* were red flags prompting me to battle: "How dare they command me. We shall see about what is going to happen."

I was not only in defensive mode but also in counter-attack mode. Neither was good for my stress levels nor for the relationship, that's for sure.

Although it may be obvious what kinds of emotions and responses these words can cause between people, what may be less obvious is the burden we put on ourselves when we use them in our self-talk. When I became aware of how many times a day, I said to myself (or to others about myself): "I **must** call Mr. Johnson. I **need** to read all my e-mails. I **should** write a new blog post," it was clear how much stress I was putting on myself.

How can this be done differently?

One tip is to use the word *choose* instead of *must, need, should,* or *ought*. It soon becomes clear which actions would give you energy and which won't.

For example,
- "I choose to call Mr. Johnson." *Well, I always like talking to him. The conversations are fun most of the time.*
- "I choose to read all my e-mails." *Pfff, that is an energy drain now. I choose to do it later so I can do something that gives me energy.*
- "I choose to write a new blog post." *Yes, I feel inspired right now. Let's do that; I already feel energized just thinking about it.*

Substituting words like *should, ought, must,* and *need* by *choose* is a very compassionate action towards yourself. It lowers your tension. As a consequence, it becomes easier to become more compassionate towards others.

Structure

The fourth aspect of Compassionate Communication is the structure of the conversation.

This structure is especially helpful in more difficult situations, both when speaking and when listening.

It consists of four steps and is based upon the Nonviolent Communication model by Marshall B. Rosenberg and the Center for Nonviolent Communication (www.cnvc.org). I altered them slightly because my experience is that it makes them flow better.

The essence of this model is to make a distinction between facts and emotions with a focus on bringing the real need or concern to the surface, plus a suggested action that can be taken to solve the need or concern.

Speaking

The four steps of the Compassionate Communication conversation structure when speaking are:
- State the objective facts that you have observed.
- Share your feeling or emotions about those facts.
- Explain the background of the feelings: the need or concern.
- Formulate a request.

This looks like this:
- "When I see or hear that …"
- "Then I feel …"
- "Because I need …"
- The request depends on what you desire:
    o Honesty: "Would you like to tell me how it felt for you what I just said?"
    o Empathy: "Would you like to tell me what you heard me say?"
    o Action: "Would you like to …?" This should be specific and doable.

If you speak with someone who knows about the inner parts or if you feel comfortable including those terms in your communication, you can adapt the steps slightly.

The four steps of the Compassionate Communication conversation structure, using the terminology of the inner parts when speaking, are:
- State the objective facts that you have observed.
- Share the feeling or emotion **that a part of you felt** about those facts.
- Explain the background of the feelings: the need or concern.
- Formulate a request.

This looks like this:
- "When I see or hear that …"
- "Then **a part in me** feels …"
- "Because **that part in me** needs …"
- The request depends on what you desire:
  - Honesty: "Would you like to tell me how it felt for you what I just said?"
  - Empathy: "Would you like to tell me what you heard me say?"
  - Action: "Would you like to …?" This should be specific and doable.

If you want to add vulnerability, you can adapt the structure to:
- "When I see or hear that …"
- "Then **a part in me** feels …"
- **"This inner part then behaves like** *Pitfall from Compassion Quadrants* **(of which I'm not proud of)"**
- "Because **that part in me** needs …"
- The request depends on what you desire:
  - Honesty: "Would you like to tell me how it felt for you what I just said?"
  - Empathy: "Would you like to tell me what you heard me say?"
  - Action: "Would you like to …?" This should be specific and doable.

Listening

When listening to someone else, you use similar steps. The big difference is that you don't know exactly what it's about. You can only work with what you observe. The other person often doesn't know their exact need or concern either. However, they do feel the tension that they want to get rid of. This often happens through complaining, venting, blaming or judging.

The invitation is first to see the behavior like an act of self-care (getting rid of tension) instead of behavior that needs to be punished and then assist them in exploring their real needs.

So, when listening, the steps of Compassionate Communication don't start with an observation of the facts, but with what the other person says.

The four steps are:
- Observation: what is said.
- Check the emotion.
- Explore the need.
- Invite the other person to formulate a request.

This looks like this:
- "I hear ..."
- "That seems to have an impact on you. Is it correct that you feel like *observed emotion*?"
- Explore the need or concern using questions like:
  o "What is needed to change this situation, so you don't have to feel *confirmed emotion* anymore?"
  o "How would you like this to be different?"
  o "Is it correct that *perceived need* is important to you?"
  o Keep asking questions until you have discovered the underlying need.
- Invite the other person to formulate a request:
  o "How could this need or concern be respected or fulfilled?"
  o "What do you need from others or yourself?"
    ▪ If it's about others: "How could you voice it in a way the other person understands your need or concern?"
    ▪ If it's about themselves: "What are you going to do for yourself?"

If you speak with someone who knows about the inner parts or if you feel comfortable including those terms in your communication, you can adapt the steps slightly.

Then the four steps are:
- Observation: what is said.
- Check the emotion **of an inner part**.
- Explore the need **of an inner part**.
- Invite the other person to formulate a request.

This looks like this:

`"I hear …"

- "That seems to have an impact on you. Is it correct that **a part of you** feels like *observed emotion*?"
- Explore the need or concern using questions like:
    - "What is needed to change this situation, so **that part in you** doesn't have to feel *confirmed emotion* anymore?"
    - "How would you like this to be different?"
    - "Is it correct that *perceived need* is important to **that part of you**?"
    - Keep asking questions until you have discovered the under-lying need.
- Invite the other person to formulate a request:
    - "How could this need or concern be respected or fulfilled?"
    - "What does **this part of you** need from others or yourself?"
        - If it is about others: "How could you voice it in a way the other person understands your need or concern?"
        - If it's about themselves: "What are you going to do for yourself?"

Gizmo Objects Inc.

As you may have noticed, Catherine has been using several aspects of Compassionate Communication throughout her interactions: attitude, openness, clarity, and words. The only aspect she hasn't used so far is structure.

When Catherine heard Frank venting about bad communication with the marketing department (see chapter 4), she first used the Compassion Technique and The ABCs of De-stressing to bring Frank to a more centered place. Then she used the Compassionate Problem Solving technique in the meeting with George, the head of marketing. In other words, she explicitly focused on the aspects of openness and clarity.

If Frank had been less upset or if there had been less time and space, she could have skipped those steps and used the four-step structure of Compassionate Communication to listen to him instead. The conversation could have been like this.

Catherine: "Frank, I hear you mention that the marketing department doesn't communicate very well. That seems to have an impact on you. Is it correct that it frustrates you?"

Frank: "It not only frustrates me; it makes me mad."

Catherine: "OK. Then it seems to have an even bigger impact on you than I thought. What is needed to change this situation, so you don't have to be mad and frustrated anymore?"

Frank: "If they would just communicate in a good way, then I would not be frustrated."

Catherine: "What would good communication look like from your point of view? What should change specifically?"

Frank: "They need to pay closer attention to the information in the e-mails they send to customers, so we don't have to deal with angry clients."

Catherine: "What went wrong in the past?"

Frank: "They put the wrong customer's service numbers in the e-mails."

Catherine: "I can see how that can cause problems. How could you voice your concern so that the marketing department could appreciate the impact it has on you?"

Frank: "That's a good question. To be honest, I always told them that they made a mistake, but never explained the magnitude of the impact it has on our team and me. I will do that."

Let's suppose that Frank knows Compassionate Communication. Then he can use the four-step structure to voice his needs to George.

Frank: "George, when I see wrong customer service numbers in the marketing e-mails, I feel frustrated because I need reliability."

Frank pauses for a second, then continues: "Would you like to tell me what you heard me say?"

George answers: "I heard you say that you are frustrated because we made an error."

Frank replies: "That's partially true, I do feel frustrated. However, I don't want to blame anyone. I want to find a solution. What's more important is that I need reliability. Would you mind listening while I explain how the wrong customer service numbers impact me, my department and the company?"

George responds: "OK. Go ahead."

Frank explains: "The way we work is like this. We have three different customer service numbers, one number for each product line. When a customer calls a number, and there is no agent available, they are put on hold. When an agent becomes available, and he notices that it's for another product line, he needs to put the customer through to the right number. There the customer can also be put on hold when there is no agent available."

When he sees George nod, Frank understands that he can continue.

"Whenever marketing announces a promotion, the service agents create a schedule to keep the waiting time to a minimum. This means that service agents of that specific product line work more hours a day and service agents from another product line take time off. When there are wrong numbers communicated, the customer who calls the wrong number ends up waiting on hold since there are fewer service agents available for that number. And since there is a promotion going on, more customers call. So, the waiting time extends. Once they end up with the right service agent, they are usually furious because they had to wait so long. And that gives my colleagues and me a lot of unnecessary stress. And it hurts the Net Promoter Score of Gizmo Objects as well."

George lets this information sink in for a moment and then says: "Thanks for clarifying this for me, Frank. Now I understand the problem. Have you already thought of a solution?"

Frank answers: "We propose to have a customer service agent make a detailed list where products and customer service telephone numbers are matched. The marketing department then uses this list as a reference when creating e-mails." Then he continues: "Would you be willing to accept this proposal?"

George responds: "That sounds like a good solution to me. Send me the list when you're ready, and I will share it immediately with the marketing team."

An example of adding vulnerability to Compassionate Communication could look like this for Frank.

> "When I see that the wrong telephone numbers are used in marketing e-mails a part in me feels rebellious and powerless at the same time. That part then behaves in a very passive way and doesn't want to pick up the phone when customers call (something that I'm not proud of). The reason is that that part in me needs reliability. Would you like to listen to my suggestion how to avoid this problem in the past and increase the reliability?"

Pitfall

Although the four steps of the structure are pretty simple, there are some pitfalls, both when listening and speaking.

In general, the conversation doesn't go very smoothly when the first three aspects are not considered: attitude, clarity and openness, and words.

More specifically, there are pitfalls to watch out for when **listening**.

The first pitfall is to step into the role of a savior: seeing the other person as a victim or as smaller, instead of an equal human being. You can change this by adapting a compassionate attitude: seeing the other person as a powerful human being who, just for this moment, needs some support.

A second pitfall is not being objective or having your own opinion about what they should do or how the situation should be.

A third pitfall is allowing the other person to digress a lot and follow them in their digressions instead of using the structure.

When it comes to **speaking** (both yourself voicing your needs or concerns and the other person answering your questions), there are many other pitfalls:

- Wanting to be right instead of pursuing happiness. This doesn't allow the real need or concern to surface.

- Blaming others or attacking them in any other way. In that case, the focus is more on what is wrong with the other person than on your own needs.

- Not willing to look at your own emotions, needs, or concerns.

- Analyzing the situation mentally instead of exploring your emotions.

- Using a quasi-feeling instead of a real feeling. A quasi-feeling is a mental analysis of the situation instead of a real emotion. This happens when the word 'feel' is followed by a word like 'that.' For example: "I have the feeling that my boss is jealous of me." When the other person uses a sentence like this, probe deeper until you discover the real emotion: "How do you feel about that?"

- Expressing the need as a strategy. Then it is about how to solve the problem instead of explaining what it's really about.

- Using a demand instead of a request. A demand causes submission or rebellion, not neutral or positive cooperation towards a solution out of free will. Requests are demands when the listener thinks that they will be punished when they are not met.

- Not making the request specific enough. The reason is usually that we assume that the other person knows what we need.

- Considering the formulation of a request as the automatic compliance of the request instead of giving the other person the freedom to choose whether or not to fulfill it. The most important goal of using the four steps is to tell the other person what is going on inside of you. I consider this a seed that is planted. It can sprout right away or later on. What is also important is that you discover what is going on inside yourself and be honest about it. This will ensure that the situation in the future will be different from the one in the past.

Extra support: Since it is not always easy to find the right words, you can find a list of emotions and needs in the free section of the Training Center on the website.

Compassionate Communication Summary

Compassionate Communication has four aspects:
- Attitude
- Openness and Clarity
- Words
- Structure

The **attitude** includes these guidelines:

- Consider the other person equal.
- Ask for permission first.
- When the other person is showing negative behavior or when you feel resistance or tension about the other person, keep this in mind:
    - It is just a primary or disowned self that is playing out.
    - All the other parts are NOT showing negative behavior.
    - There is an imbalance between a primary and disowned self.

To be able to be more **open** and provide more **clarity**, these are a few actions you can do to prepare for the conversation:

- Apply the Compassion Technique with the other person in mind.
- Create a Double Compassion Quadrant of yourself and the other person.
- Formulate the problem as a driver statement like in Compassionate Problem Solving.

These are **words** to avoid:

- War-like words;
- *Yes, but* and *but* (replace it by *and*);
- Exaggerations like *never* and *always*;
- *Should, ought, must* and *need* (replace them by *choose*).

The **structure** of the Compassionate Communication conversation is slightly different between speaking and listening.

In general, the four steps of the Compassionate Communication conversation structure when speaking are (they can be slightly adapted when addressing inner parts):
- State the objective facts that you have observed.
- Share your feelings or emotions about those facts.
- Explain the background of the feelings: the need or concern.
- Formulate a request.

The four steps when listening are:
- Observation: what is said.
- Check the emotion.
- Explore the need.
- Invite the other person to formulate a request.

It is not necessary to take all four aspects of Compassionate Communication into account all at once. However, the more aspects you use, the more compassionate your communication will be. However, using one or two aspects might already make a big difference when compared with the past. I invite you to start with the aspect that is the easiest for you and then add more as required.

Action for Self-Care

Compassionate Communication is for situations with *interpersonal* tension. Self-care is an action you take when you experience *personal* tension.

However, sometimes you need Compassionate Communication to voice to others how you are going to take care of yourself.

After finding out what the root of the personal tension is, you might have concluded that there is something out of balance. For example, you are working too hard, your work is not giving you enough satisfaction, or you are adapting too much to other people's needs.

If that is the case, you might want to take some action for self-care. For example:

- When you are working too hard, you might want to block some time in your calendar to relax.
- If your work is no longer challenging, you might consider redistributing the work within the team, so there is more room for aspects of your work that give you energy. Or even change jobs or companies.
- When you are adapting too much to the needs of other people, you might want to co-create agreements or have someone help you prepare for situations that are difficult for you (for example when talking to customers or discussing a team member's performance).

If other people are involved (like in the second and third example), Compassionate Communication is used to communicate this act of self-care to bring the message across in the right way and avoid misunderstandings. Another approach is that the act of self-care is addressed in a meeting using Compassionate Problem Solving.

Key Take-Aways

The fourth and last step of the D.U.E.T. process consists of taking action in some way.

This means:

- For interpersonal tension: Compassionate Communication.
- For practical or process tension: Applying the proposal from a Compassionate Problem Solving session.
- For personal tension: Action for self-care or Compassionate Communication if you need to share this action with others.

As you have noticed in the past chapters, my intention with the D.U.E.T. process is not to offer a rigid framework or process that needs to be strictly followed, but a collection of techniques to transform tensions and raise the vibe.

One example of the flexibility of the D.U.E.T. process is that Compassionate Communication can be used at any moment. It is not necessary to first go through steps 2 (understand and solve the tension) and 3 (embrace and transform the root of the tension) of the D.U.E.T. process before you can apply Compassionate Communication.

Compassionate Communication consists of four aspects: attitude, openness and clarity, words and structure.

Since it's not always easy to find the right words when using the four-step Compassionate Communication structure, you can find a list with emotions and needs in the free section of the Training Center on the website.

The result of applying Compassionate Communication and other techniques of the D.U.E.T. framework is that (mental) space is created for you and your team, and that the vibe is raised. As a consequence, solutions to deal with your own specific challenges will pop up more easily. For example, when tensions arise with new software, new office designs, new ways of working, or when other changes are introduced.

Another benefit of knowing and using the D.U.E.T. process is not only having techniques to transform tensions. It also offers a reference frame and a common language. For example, when every team member knows the Compassion Quadrants technique, another team member might say: "I notice you keep having conflicts with our manager. Why don't we use the Compassion Quadrants to find out what it's really all about." Or before or during a meeting, the person who is leading it can say: "We all know this is a rather delicate subject. Let's all do the Compassion Technique first." The benefit is that there is less blaming, less defensiveness, more openness, faster transforming of tensions, and a quicker process to raise the vibe.

Chapter 10

Compassionate Leadership in Action: Facilitating Vibe Transitions

As you have read in the previous chapters, the four-step D.U.E.T. process is an excellent framework to transform tensions. In this chapter, we will explore further how to use it to raise the vibe.

In my opinion, this is the most important task before doing anything else. First, it will raise the level of performance and well-being. And secondly, it will make team members more resilient when changes happen. Change always includes a separation and grieving phase. For most people, this is experienced as a negative tension. Having tools and techniques at your disposal, like the ones from the D.U.E.T. framework, will help from spiraling down to or getting stuck in a negative vibe.

In this chapter, you will also be presented with extra tips about what you can do as a leader to facilitate yourself and your team to raise the vibe. In other words, this chapter focuses on Compassionate Leadership in action.

The approach we take is to focus on what is necessary for each transition. This means: what is necessary to make the transition from the negative to the neutral vibe, from the neutral to the positive vibe and from the positive to the inspiring vibe.

Before we do that, there are a few things to keep in mind.

- The techniques from a lower vibe are still necessary for a higher vibe. For example, although the Compassion Technique is particularly helpful to help people raise their center of gravity from the negative to the neutral vibe, it can't be left out when working with a person or team that has its center of gravity in the positive vibe. The reason is that vibes fluctuate. In every person's life, some circumstances bring the vibe down. Then it's crucial to have the right tools and techniques to bounce back quickly.

- Techniques for a higher vibe can't always be applied to a lower vibe. For example, when the vibe is negative or neutral, this shows itself in deficient communication. Usually, organizations want to cure this with communication training. However, when people are deeply immersed in the negative vibe, there is not enough willingness to look at communication issues with colleagues and not enough safety to reflect on themselves. That is one of the reasons why a communication training or change projects in general don't reach their goals: techniques that are only suited for the positive and inspiring vibe are applied to people in the negative or neutral vibe.

- Growth occurs naturally (including the rise of the vibe), and wisdom reveals itself organically unless there are barriers present. So, the goal is to use moments of tension to detect and remove those barriers. When that happens, usually insights and solutions suddenly start popping up. Techniques of the D.U.E.T. process are used to remove those barriers by transforming the corresponding tensions. The more this is combined with Compassionate Leadership, the better the results. However, the specific ways in which Compassionate Leadership is applied differ from transition to transition. So, it's not one size fits all.

From a Negative to a Neutral Vibe

As a reminder, people who are in a negative vibe have the following characteristics.

People in a negative vibe can be recognized by their behavior. They complain a lot, blame others behind their back and gossip. People in a negative vibe say they will do something, but afterward often don't follow through on their promises. There is a lot of (often irrational) resistance. Personal failures are covered up, and promises are broken. They have a lot of excuses and reasons why something can't be done. For people in a negative vibe, hoarding knowledge equals power. In other words, they hardly share any information, knowledge, or wisdom. They are also too afraid to share anything personal. They are focused on protecting themselves. The rules are bent or violated, if needed, to achieve that goal.

When it comes to collaboration, people in a negative vibe will only do this when it is forced upon them or necessary to protect themselves. They are reluctant to work together with new people or people who are different from them. Colleagues who are in another vibe are often sabotaged in some way.

When change happens, they are more focused on what can go wrong. This is because they are afraid they might lose something. They are focused on "what's in it for *me*," primarily to protect what they have.

When you look at their availability, they are absent both mentally and physically for a considerable amount of time. They take long toilet or smoke breaks. Absenteeism because of sick leave is also high, with potentially high costs for their employer. Mentally they are often not present. They spend a lot of time discussing worst-case scenarios, both in their head and with other people who are usually also in a negative vibe.

Their feeling of safety is very low. As a result, lots of time goes into protecting themselves from potential danger. This can be protective behavior when interacting with someone (like not cooperating in a meeting), but also being on the lookout where potential risk might be present (like hanging around water coolers a lot to pick up the latest news). It can also mean checking out social media during the day to make sure they are on top of anything negative that might happen.

Their feeling of being supported is also very low. Colleagues or managers are not available to help them — at least that's the perception of people in a negative vibe. Since their focus is on possible negative things that might happen, it becomes a self-fulfilling prophecy. If the glass is half full, they will perceive it as half empty and complain about it. Often people in a negative vibe are stuck in a negative vortex. This negative vibe usually repels people who are in another vibe, which leads to the self-fulfilling conclusion that nobody wants to help them. From an organizational point of view, the investment in people with a negative vibe is usually low. Only mandatory training is provided.

In a negative vibe, feedback is focused on what people do wrong. This contributes to the feeling of not being supported.

The energy in the office or work floor feels heavy and pessimistic. As a result, talented people won't come on board.

As a reminder, people who are in a **neutral vibe** have the following characteristics.

The behavior of people in a neutral vibe is somewhat different from the negative vibe. Although the vibe is still low, it is not as toxic.

They still complain, gossip and blame others behind their back once in a while, but that is usually when they are in contact with people in a negative vibe. More than any other vibe, they adapt to the vibe of others. They do this to belong to the group. This gives them safety. The result is that they often put their own opinion aside if that is necessary to belong.

People in a neutral vibe usually follow through on their promises. They make sure that their work is done, but nothing more. They don't proactively seek better solutions or help out others when they have finished their tasks. Rules and formal agreements are their standards. That's what gives them a feeling of security.

Personal failures are still covered up, especially if they could lead to exclusion from the group. They share more information, knowledge, and wisdom than people in a negative vibe, but again with the underlying motive of being included or not being excluded. They are also not keen on sharing personal feelings, only superficial experiences like what they read in the paper or watched on television.

When it comes to collaboration, they tend to work together more than people in a negative vibe. The driver could be the need to be included, but also because they feel some kind of responsibility. They are still not very keen on working with people who are different, but they are less reluctant than people in a negative vibe.

When someone asks for help, they will first see if it fits their schedule. That can change if they feel they might be excluded by not helping. That's why they tend to proactively help people in some kind of power position, whether it's formal or informal, rather than one of their peers.

When change happens, they are more focused on what could go wrong, instead of the potential benefits of the new situation. They look for "what's in it for *me*" from the point of not being excluded and "what's in it for *us*" to protect the achievement of the (small) group they belong to.

People in a neutral vibe are more available than people in a negative vibe. They take regular breaks, and the rate of absenteeism due to sick leave is the average of the industry. However, mentally, they are not completely present. They're – unconsciously – still on the lookout for potential threats.

Their feeling of safety is medium. Still, a fair amount of time goes to protecting themselves from potential (psychological) danger, especially when the vibe can turn any time to negative.

Their feeling of being supported is also medium. They feel that they are supported by their colleagues and managers, but usually only when they proactively ask for it or when circumstances force it (like illnesses in the team). Organizations tend to offer more formal support to people in a neutral vibe than to people in a negative vibe. Initiatives that are taken by their employer include workshops to improve effectivity and efficiency, plus (often only superficial) team building events.

In a neutral vibe, feedback is focused on improving people's weaknesses. Their talents and positive qualities might also be mentioned, but the focus is on their flaws. The danger is that this might push them towards a negative vibe.

The energy in the office or work floor is neutral. It is not heavy or pessimistic, but also not positive or stimulating. Talented people might come on board but usually, leave the team or organization after a while.

What do people need to make the transition to a neutral vibe?

When we look at Maslow's Hierarchy of Needs, this transition is about the transition from physiological and safety needs (level 1 and 2) to belonging needs (level 3).

The most important step is to feel more safe and secure in interacting with other people. In the first instance, belonging means not being *excluded*. Later on, in the neutral vibe spectrum, this can evolve into being *included*.

Only when people feel safe enough, will they be open enough to look at their own behavior and make changes.

When people in a negative vibe show resistance to change, it is not necessarily about the new conditions, but about not feeling safe and secure enough.

They are not demanding a lot of personal growth opportunities and training courses. However, when they are provided with some kind of formal support, they feel respected.

Techniques to make this transition

From the D.U.E.T. framework, the two most important techniques to make this transition are:

- The Compassion Technique
- The ABCs of De-stressing

The Compassion Technique helps people to get in a neutral or even positive state when there is a conflict with someone else or when they feel limited by someone else. The ABCs of De-stressing can be used for any situation where stress is experienced.

In chapter 7, you saw how Frank was helped by using the Compassion Technique and The ABCs of De-stressing.

What is important in both techniques is that people don't have to tell anyone what is going on inside them. When applying the Compassion Technique, they don't have to give details about which tension they experience with whom. They don't need to explain what gives them stress in The ABCs of De-stressing.

Not having to tell anyone what it's about, provides safety. This means that both techniques can be applied, not only with individuals but also with groups with a negative vibe.

That's why they are the best tools to use for this transition.

What you can do as a leader to facilitate this transition

Since people in the negative vibe are looking out for potential threats the whole time, it's important to provide a secure base for them amidst all other things that are going on. As a leader, you can be that secure base.

Let's look at some specific actions you can take for this transition.

First, make sure you are not in a negative vibe yourself. If so, use the Compassion Technique or the ABCs of De-stressing yourself before coaching other people.

What people need to make the transition from a negative to a neutral vibe, is stability and predictability. Showing predictable and calm behavior as a leader might be enough for them, even if there is lots of uncertainty in the rest of the organization.

It is not always easy to lead an individual or a group with a negative vibe especially when there is a lot of negative behavior like complaining, gossiping, and blaming others.

The first step you can take is perceiving negative behavior in another way: as a way to take care of themselves by releasing tensions. In other words, look at it as good self-care on the one hand and an opportunity to find the cause of the tension, on the other hand.

The second step you can take is to look at the long-term potential of each individual. Take a step back and see which talents each of them has, beyond their current negative behavior. Whenever an outburst of negative energy happens, take their long-term potential or core talent into account. This helps not to be overwhelmed when there is a vortex of negative energy that sucks in the whole team, including yourself.

One of the reasons why people have their center of gravity in the negative vibe or reside there once in a while is the feeling that they didn't get the respect they deserved.

A very common behavior that is not respectful nor compassionate is providing unsolicited advice. Although most people's intention behind unsolicited advice is good, it can create a lot of resistance.

However, a lot of times, it is helpful or even necessary to share advice or instructions. One of the characteristics of people who are in a negative vibe is that they are so focused on avoiding threats that they have a very limited vision of what is needed or what is possible. As a result, people in a negative vibe need more guidance and suggestions than people in other vibes. But they are less open to it. So how do you deal with this situation?

What you can do instead of sharing unsolicited advice is ask for permission to share a thought or an idea. This not only shows respect, but it also gets the other person out of their current thinking pattern. And only when they permit you, can you share your insights. A major pitfall here is to use a sentence like "Can I share an insight with you?" without waiting for an answer and still use it as an excuse to share advice in an unsolicited way. This triggers the same defense mechanisms and creates resistance in the other person.

Another reason why people end up in a negative vibe is that they feel power-less. They feel that they have no choice. They feel that they don't have any control over nor can influence topics that impact them.

A first step that can be taken is supporting them in seeing what they *do* have control over and what they *can* influence. When they see what is in their power the feeling of powerlessness decreases, even if it's about making rather simple choices.

A second step is adopting a new way of making decisions by using consent. Since this will be easier when people are in a neutral vibe, this will be explained in the next transition.

People also tend to get into a negative vibe if they are given instructions without knowing the reason behind it or without seeing the bigger picture. What you can do as a leader is to provide a brief explanation of the reason behind the decisions. This reduces the feeling of insecurity and powerlessness. However, don't get into too many details because people in a negative vibe are not open to hearing them (yet).

Another reason for people being in a negative vibe is that they hadn't had the chance to grieve over one or more separations when a change occurred (remember the bonding cycle). In today's world, changes take place one after the other with ever-increasing speed. In many cases, people go through the bonding cycle automatically, especially when it's about small changes or when there was an attachment, but not a bond. However, in some situations, there was a strong emotional bond or the change had a lot of impact on an individual, team, or organization. If that's the case, it might be necessary to slow down, make time and space for the grief phase and support them going through it.

Last but not least, use Compassionate Communication yourself. Don't expect people in the negative vibe to be able to do this (yet). They need to be in at least a neutral vibe to apply this. But you can support them getting there by using it in your conversations like Catherine from Gizmo Objects.

From a Neutral to a Positive Vibe

As a reminder, people who are in a positive vibe have the following characteristics.

When people are in a positive vibe, they are motivated to perform and open for feedback to increase their skills, abilities, and knowledge. Gossiping and blaming others behind their back doesn't happen too often. The reason is that they feel safer to address the underlying issues. They feel more secure, and their self-esteem is high enough.

They are less focused on protecting the current status quo and more on new opportunities which may present themselves. They are goal-oriented. This can be a personal goal, a team goal, or the purpose of the organization. They understand that to reach their objectives change is a necessary factor. However, sometimes, they are so focused on their personal or team goal that they lose sight of the purpose of the organization and don't take the impact on the ecosystem into account.

From the positive vibe on, people are more focused on intrinsic motivation. In his book *Drive*, author Dan Pink states that the three key components are purpose, mastery, and autonomy. The purpose is the feeling of doing something meaningful. It is the feeling that there is a relevant contribution. Mastery is the desire to improve. Someone who seeks mastery needs to attain it for its own sake. Autonomy is the need to direct your own life and work. To be fully motivated, you must be able to control what you do, when you do it, and who you do it with.

People in a positive vibe are not keen on failing or sharing personal errors. However, they know that addressing those errors could help them improve. Since their own development is more important than protecting themselves, they are willing to look at their mistakes, unhelpful behavior, or limiting patterns. However, the environment still needs to be safe enough. This usually means a one-on-one session with a manager, coach, or therapist. For deep introspection, when colleagues are present, a special setting is needed like an intensive team building weekend or a personal growth seminar. But even then, they only really open up to people they trust.

People in a positive vibe look for ways to collaborate. They know that sharing knowledge and information equals multiplying it. They are focused on team results and cheer each other on. They are focused on "what's in it for *me*" from the point of personal development and "what's in it for the *team*" to support achieving a bigger goal. The team can be their own team, but also the department or the whole organization. That's why they have a positive outlook on change and change projects. Rules and formal agreements are deemed necessary to have a framework to work in or to start from, but they can be changed if required after deliberation.

They are highly available. They take very short or no breaks during the day and take almost no sick leave.

Their feeling of safety is high. As a result, only a small portion of their time goes to protecting themselves. They are mentally and physically present at work most of the time.

Their feeling of being supported is also high. There is an emphasis on helping each other. Their manager acts as a coach, and proactively seeks a way to support their team. Internal or external coaches are also available to support team members in their personal growth. The organization further invests in these employees by providing a personal development plan and by organizing team-building initiatives that are focused on creating more self-awareness.

In a positive vibe, feedback is focused on how to strengthen talents and core qualities. While weaknesses might also be detected and improvements might be included in a development plan, the focus is on their strengths.

The energy in the office or work floor is positive and stimulating. Talented people are attracted to teams with a positive vibe. However, they will sometimes leave when they get a better job offer elsewhere. This might mean a better wage, more benefits, or the opportunity to work in an environment with an inspiring vibe.

What do people need to make the transition to a positive vibe?

When we look at Maslow's Hierarchy of Needs, this transition is about the transition from belonging needs (level 3) to esteem needs (level 4).

People in a neutral vibe are in between the negative and positive vibe. This means they can go down (again) to the negative vibe when something impactful happens. The reason why I'm mentioning this is that many change projects are focusing on a new and exciting future (in this way hinting to the positive vibe), without taking potential insecurities and the bonding cycle into account.

The result is that an individual or team might end up in a negative vibe instead of the expected and sought-after positive vibe.

In other words, it is still very important to keep aspects of psychological safety into account. When it was in the transition from a negative to a neutral vibe primarily about not being excluded (which transforms into being included during the mid and late phase of the neutral vibe), in this transition from a neutral to a positive vibe, it's about being valued for your skills, ideas or other contributions.

In this transition from a neutral to a positive vibe, it is not only about being valued as a team member, but also about valuing other team members. This also means discovering the differences between oneself and other people in order to avoid misunderstandings and create meaningful relationships.

Techniques to make this transition

From the D.U.E.T. framework, the three most important techniques to be used to make this transition as an individual are:

- Compassionate Problem Solving
- Compassionate Communication
- Compassion Quadrants

The value of formulating a driver statement (part of the Compassionate Problem Solving technique) is that when tension is perceived, the impact on an individual, a team, or the organization is expressed. This puts tensions in a larger or more objective perspective. When that is combined with consent decision-making, lots of the negative aspects of traditional meetings and decision-making are transformed into meaningful and even energizing moments.

Consent decision-making ensures that people who might be affected by a proposal to solve a problem or tension, have an impact on the outcome. This is very empowering. On the other hand, consent decision-making avoids both power plays of more dominant people (command and control) and long exhausting meetings where everybody has to agree (consensus). This means that lots of decisions can be made in a short time frame.

When we make the link with Gizmo Objects then we saw in chapter 7 how Compassionate Problem Solving helped Frank to solve the practical tension of the wrong telephone numbers in e-mails. In chapter 8, we learned how Compassion Quadrants helped him to understand why he is having issues with his colleague Marc and how to resolve them. In chapter 9, we were presented with Catherine and Frank's use of Compassionate Communication.

The techniques that were most important for the transition from a negative to a neutral vibe (The Compassion Technique and The ABCs of De-stressing) are still important in this transition. Once people start communicating more with others, some stress can show up. To stay in the neutral vibe and not go down to the negative vibe, these techniques come in handy.

What you can do as a leader to facilitate this transition

For leaders, tips from the previous transition still apply, but they get different accents in this transition from a neutral to a positive vibe.

In the previous transition, it was important to be predictable and calm for people to feel safe. Now, it becomes more important for them to feel supported in their personal growth.

This starts with sharing how you see their long-term potential and their core talents. While you used this picture *for yourself* in the previous transition to keep your eyes on the power in each individual when they show negative behavior, in this transition you voice their talents and core qualities *towards them*. As a leader, you express the bigger vision you have of them. And you remind each of your team members of this vision, especially when they are going through a tough time (so they don't descend to the negative vibe) or when they are taking on a new challenging project (to get or keep them in the positive vibe).

When people have their center of gravity in a neutral vibe, they are in-between the negative and positive vibe. And often they fluctuate between them. One day they perceive the glass as half empty, the next day as half full. When you want to support them to go to the positive vibe, keep inviting them to look at the half-full glass. It's about supporting them to keep the positive in mind as well, instead of only the negative. This doesn't mean to be blind to pitfalls, but to look at those pitfalls from a safe and problem-solving position instead of being overwhelmed by the negative aspects.

While asking for permission is still the first thing to do, this transition is less about sharing your advice and guidelines. It becomes more about asking the right questions to get your team members thinking and coming up with solutions and ideas themselves.

Explaining the why and the bigger picture of where the team or organization is heading remains important. While the idea of sharing the bigger picture in the previous transition was to provide enough safety, now it's more about visualizing the way forward.

This also shows in the bonding cycle. The emphasis is now on attaching and bonding with the new situation. However, it remains important to keep the separation and grieving phase in mind and to create enough time and space for it. If not, then individuals or the team can spiral down to the negative vibe instead of up to the positive one.

Compassionate Problem Solving is used to find solutions in a fast, constructive way without creating new tensions or renewing old ones. Compassionate Communication becomes important for everybody to understand each other and avoid misinterpretations. It is used to voice one's own needs and concerns in daily work and to detect the needs and concerns of others. As a leader, it is important to be an example.

From a Positive to an Inspiring Vibe

As a reminder, people who are in an inspiring vibe have the following characteristics.

People in an inspiring vibe are motivated and eager to perform and contribute. They are not only open to feedback to increase their skills, abilities, and knowledge, but are proactively looking for it. They know it benefits them and the organization.

They have a high level of self-esteem, but it is different from people in the positive vibe where it is often dominantly present. For people in the positive vibe, it often is a protection mechanism. It protects them from being confronted with their shadow side. In the inspiring vibe, people know that to grow as a person, these shadow sides need to be included. They look for their blind spots — and feel safe enough to do so together with the team. They know that in those shadows, the blocks are hidden that prevent functioning in an optimal and balanced way. Or the other way around, they know that the shadows can hide the greatest treasures for a rich and fulfilling life.

People in an inspiring vibe are motivated by contributing to a compelling purpose. That's why they can predominantly be found in startups or organizations that are focused on the greater good for the planet or humanity. Mastery and autonomy are essential.

They look for continuous improvement on all levels, for quantitative and qualitative growth, both as an individual and organization. That's why they constantly look for supportive technology and personal development tools and techniques. They know that rules and formal agreements need to change continuously to keep up with an ever-changing environment and have incorporated a safe and clear way of doing this in their daily work. They ask themselves questions like "How could I be wrong regarding this topic?" while in the other vibes people tend to defend their own ideas and opinions.

From a collaboration point of view, sharing information and knowledge is taken to the next level. Co-creation is embedded and highly stimulated. There is also a genuine interest in helping other people not only with ideas, suggestions, and practical solutions but also with discovering blocks and opportunities to grow as a person. They know that the process of assisting another person in embracing their shadow side is an enriching experience for them as well. That's why deep personal issues are shared frequently at work and not only in separate retreats or workshops. They are focused on "what is in it for the *ecosystem*" because they know everything is interconnected. They know that contributions to any involved stakeholder help to lift all parties, including themselves.

Contrary to what you might expect, they are less available than people in a positive vibe. They take more breaks during the day because they know it is necessary to recharge from time to time to keep functioning optimally. That's why they also take more time off from work to focus on activities, places, and people that fuel them in any way: physically, mentally, emotionally, or spiritually. That way, they prevent the specific kind of burnout from the positive vibe, which is related to working too hard.

Their feeling of safety is very high. As a result, almost no time is spent on protecting themselves. They are 100 percent present at work and show their vulnerability.

Their feeling of being supported is also very high. Since there is co-creation, they feel supported by their peers. Coaching by a manager or an internal or external coach is replaced by peer-to-peer coaching. Everybody has learned coaching skills because there's no time to wait for a coach or therapist. The organization is focused on enabling them to the fullest. The right technology, environment, and facilities are provided, together with a constant feedback loop on how to improve this support.

In an inspiring vibe, feedback is focused on enquiring how people can become a better version of themselves and asking what they need to accomplish it.

The energy in the office or work floor is exciting and energizing. As a result, top talent can't wait to be part of a team with an inspiring vibe. Moreover, they will stay, even when they receive offers with a larger wage or more benefits. If they decide to leave, whether it is to start their own company or to work for another team with an inspiring vibe, they will be the most fanatic ambassadors who can't wait to come to the yearly alumni event.

What do people need to make the transition to an inspiring vibe?

When we look at Maslow's Hierarchy of Needs, it's about the transition from esteem needs (level 4) to self-actualization needs (level 5).

This transition is harder to make than the previous ones. It's new to the workplace and requires a lot of vulnerability. However, the rewards are high as well.

To thrive in the inspiring vibe and to be inspiring to others, personal limitations need to be conquered. It's about vulnerability. It's about being willing and able to look at one's shadow sides and integrate them. Vulnerability is necessary for people to bond with each other. Without bonding, it is impossible to inspire someone else.

This applies to leaders, but also to all people in the inspiring vibe. Everybody becomes a leader in this vibe, not out of a title, but out of a way of being. This is necessary to unleash the full power of a team. The manager can't be the limiting factor anymore.

This also means that leaders must give up parts of their role. It means giving up elements that were important for one's identity, like a title or control over every decision. It means rediscovering oneself and possibly going through an intense separation and grieving phase (see the bonding cycle). Since this is also rather new, not many leaders truly succeed in doing this (yet). As a result, they limit their team or organization. They put – unconsciously – a ceiling on the positive vibe, keeping the inspiring vibe out of reach. Unless they take action and do whatever is needed to reach the inspiring level themselves and become a truly Compassionate Leader. In chapter 11 you will find a pathway that shows how to become one.

The inspiring vibe is where true self-managing teams reside. This is characterized by continuous peer-to-peer coaching. Both on the level of skills and ideas and the level of deep self-discovery. However, this is not easy for most people.

Many people who are invited or (gently) forced to work in a self-managing or self-regulating environment suddenly experience more personal tensions. Their primary selves might go in overdrive to protect them or their disowned selves might ask for more attention. The disowned selves could add some necessary positive qualities to the mix if they would get more space. At the same time, the primary selves might resist this. Some of the causes are fear for failure, fear for success, or fear for their greatness. This causes personal tensions. That's why they first need techniques to solve their personal tension like the ABCs of De-stressing and then other techniques to detect their inner selves and balance them like the Compassion Quadrants and the Inner Balance Technique.

Techniques to make this transition

From the D.U.E.T. framework, the two most important techniques to be used to make this transition as an individual are:

- Compassion Quadrants
- Inner Balance Technique

As you saw in the previous transition, Compassion Quadrants help to get more insights into the dynamics between another person and yourself. This helps to make the transition from a neutral to a positive vibe. They also open a gateway towards discovering your shadow sides that ask for attention. In that respect, Compassion Quadrants are a great preparation for the Inner Balance Technique.

In the Inner Balance Technique, parts in us that simultaneously step on the gas pedal and the brake, causing us not to reach our goals, are balanced. The part that was in the shadow and was pressing on the brake and was limiting us is transformed into a supportive part. The consequence is that we not only press the gas pedal and accelerate; we don't have to press the gas pedal so hard anymore to reach the goals. Consequently, one of the causes of burnout of people in a positive vibe is avoided. While one of the major causes of burnout in a negative vibe is being overwhelmed, the cause in a positive vibe is pushing the gas pedal too long (and usually with the brake on at the same time).

When we make the link with Gizmo Objects, then we saw in chapter 8 how the Compassion Quadrants helped Frank in changing his perception towards his colleague Marc and how the Inner Balance Technique supported the self-development of both of them.

The techniques that were most important for the previous transitions still apply as well. The Compassion Technique and The ABCs of De-stressing are still useful when stress comes up in the self-discovery process. Compassionate Problem Solving is still the way to process practical tensions quickly. And Compassionate Communication becomes an invaluable tool in daily conversations and in peer-to-peer coaching.

What you can do as a leader to facilitate this transition

For leaders, tips from the previous transitions still apply, but they get different accents in this transition from a positive to an inspiring vibe.

In the first transition, it was important to be predictable and calm to make people feel safe. In the second transition, it was important to support them in their personal growth. Now, it has become more important to show your own shadow sides and vulnerability. By being a role model, you inspire your team to pursue the path of self-discovery and vulnerability.

The more leaders allow themselves to be in touch with their whole being, including shadow sides, the more they feel a personal safety. The more leaders feel safe, the more they can offer safety to others: the more safety, the more vulnerability. The more vulnerability, the faster tensions can be faced and solved. The more safety and vulnerability, the faster people open up and bond.

The long-term potential and core talents of your team members remain focus points. The difference with the previous transition is that now it is important to support them in discovering the inner blocks that keep them away from reaching their full potential (using Compassion Quadrants) and help them with balancing their core talents with what is hidden in the shadows (using the Inner Balance Technique).

Asking the right questions, so your team members come up with solutions and ideas themselves, is still very beneficial. What is added in this transition is that sometimes you only need to be present with them to have the wisdom emerge from within. In other words, you don't have to prepare questions anymore or know a lot yourself. You just allow the wisdom to reveal itself. This can mean that you still get inspired to ask a specific question, but also that you remain silent and hold the space for the other person so they can come up with their own insights or ideas.

In this transition, explaining the why and the bigger picture shifts to being open to challenging questions and investigating blind spots. The bonding cycle keeps playing an essential role. Since grieving is crucial to attach to a new situation and be fully engaged, this phase needs to be checked for every change. And, if necessary, the right amount of space and time needs to be allocated to go through this phase.

Compassionate Communication becomes the way team members communicate with each other. In this way, tensions are detected right away and don't get the chance to build up or mix with other tensions. This ensures a very agile, efficient, and effective way of working and a faster way to spot opportunities.

And when the team has made a successful transition to the inspiring vibe, the most important thing to do as a leader is to get out of their way. Of course, you can still be there as a soundboard, a facilitator, a coach of coaches, and a role model. Or you can design a new role for yourself.

Key Take-Aways

As a leader, you probably want to improve the performance and well-being of your team by supporting them to raise their vibe.

In this chapter, three transitions were discussed: from a negative to a neutral vibe, from a neutral to a positive vibe and from a positive to an inspiring vibe.

It's important to note that each transition requires a different approach. Techniques from a previous transition are still helpful for the next one, but not the other way around. One of the pitfalls is to use the wrong approach and techniques. For example, the techniques for a transition from a neutral to a positive vibe, while the individual or team is in a negative vibe, might not have the desired effect. Another pitfall is to think that only the techniques from the D.U.E.T. framework for that specific transition are needed. For example, when going from a positive to an inspiring vibe, The ABCs of De-stressing still needs to be used when a stress peak or loss of control is experienced.

To make the transition from the **negative to the neutral vibe,** people need to feel safe and secure. That is the most important part. Techniques that can be used to facilitate this transition are the Compassion Technique and The ABCs of De-stressing.

What you can do as a leader to support individuals or teams going through this transition, is offer stability and predictability, take the long-term potential of every individual into account, refrain from giving unsolicited advice, show them options and share the bigger picture behind decisions. Sometimes it might be necessary to take a step back and allow time and space to go through the grieving phase of the bonding cycle.

To make the transition from a **neutral to a positive vibe,** people need both enough safety (in order not to end up in a negative vibe) and a vision to move forward. Techniques that can be used to facilitate this transition are Compassionate Problem Solving, Compassionate Communication, and Compassion Quadrants.

As a leader, you can support individuals and teams going through this transition by voicing the long-term vision you have for them, keep their focus on the benefits of the change, ask questions to get the team thinking for itself and keep sharing the bigger picture behind decisions. In the bonding cycle, the emphasis is on attaching and bonding with the new situation, but it remains important to make space for the separation and grieving phases.

To make the transition from the **positive to the inspiring vibe,** people need to focus on self-actualization. This means pursuing their dreams on the one hand and making room for growth on the other. This room is created by facing and integrating their shadow sides or disowned selves. Being vulnerable is a requirement for this. It is also a requirement for deep bonding. Without bonding, it is impossible to really inspire someone.

Techniques that can be used to facilitate this transition are Compassion Quadrants and the Inner Balance Technique.

As a leader, it is even more important to be a role model than in the previous transitions. This means being open and vulnerable. It means being able to be present without knowing the answers. It means being a coach, a facilitator and a midwife for the people of your team — especially when they embark on their journey of self-discovery.

Chapter 11

Becoming a Compassionate Leader

As you have read throughout this book, it is crucial to have leaders, coaches, or other people who are Compassionate Leaders in your organization to transform tensions to raise the vibe.

This means that Compassionate Leaders raise their vibe and balancing their own inner parts first. The latter is especially important in creating enough inner safety to be vulnerable.

This can be done by applying the techniques from the D.U.E.T. process on themselves. Then it becomes much easier to facilitate others.

In this chapter, you will be shown a pathway to becoming a (more) Compassionate Leader. And as a summary of all the tips that were shared throughout the book, you will be presented with the habits of Compassionate Leaders.

But before we dive into the pathway and the habits, let's first go back to the characteristics of a Compassionate Leader.

In general, a Compassionate Leader is someone who:

- Knows what compassion is — and is not — and lives accordingly;
- Acts as a secure base for their team;
- Considers tension a pointer to opportunities for growth;
- Focuses on increasing the level of Compassionate Leadership: the ability to take individuals, teams, and organizations to a higher vibe, which is a higher level of performance and well-being, in a safe and stimulating way when tensions occur.

A Compassionate Leader is also someone:

- Who is open-minded.
- Who balances:
    - o Masculine and feminine energy in themselves;
    - o Doing and being;
    - o Technology/results and humaneness/connections;

- o Down-to-earthiness and spirituality;
- o Fun and getting stuff done.
- Who is curious about differences and offers a safe space for them to be present.
- Who looks for clarity and the essence and root of the matter.
- Who is vulnerable, which is a source of strength when being present with someone.
- Who listens with compassion and speaks from the heart. This doesn't mean that it's soft or fluffy, Compassionate Leaders can be very direct at addressing pain or tension and point people to their responsibility; the difference is that they do this with compassion.
- Who first looks to raise the center of gravity of the vibe of an individual or team and only then announces changes.
- Who quickly raises the vibe again when it goes down due to change projects or other events.

The result is that they are not only more successful and loved by their teams, but experience a lot of freedom in their lives as well. They are not dependent anymore on other people's approval. They are free from the opinions and judgments of other people. They are free from patterns that hold them back. They are free from fears.

The term *free* also means that all those elements can still show up, but Compassionate Leaders are not taken hostage by them. Those elements don't shake up their world. Compassionate Leaders can be present in stressful situations, with people in victim mode and with uncertainty. They can deal with life with a compassionate attitude. In this way, they provide solutions for themselves, the people they work with, and their organizations. They make way for options that nobody thought of before.

By being who they are and by living compassionately, they invite others – unconsciously – to become Compassionate Leaders as well. They inspire by being.

Leading by example can also mean making mistakes, admitting them, choosing something else, and talking about their process. In other words, a Compassionate Leader is also someone who hasn't ticked all the boxes yet but has the heart-felt desire to follow this path and become a genuine Compassionate Leader.

Compassionate Leaders also have a higher level of consciousness. Let's explore what that means.

Leaders and the Growth of Consciousness

In chapter 1, we looked at the characteristics of the four vibes. An individual or team can grow to a higher one or can fall back to a lower vibe. Let's tie this to how we grow up as human beings.

Human beings go through several stages: from a baby to a toddler to a child to an adolescent to an adult.

These stages are also characterized by development in consciousness.

As a baby, the world is small. Parents, family, and neighbors are the only people around. Then more and more people enter the child's world: other children in school, teachers, people they encounter on the streets and in shops, sports teams and hobby associations. This continues when the child becomes an adult. The world becomes larger and larger, and the view of the individual develops.

In psychology, there are three main stages: pre-conventional, conventional, and post-conventional. Other names are egocentric, ethnocentric or socio-centric, and world-centric.

In the **pre-conventional or egocentric stage,** the focus is on oneself. A baby needs to be egocentric to survive. It needs parents for care and safety. This is a ME dynamic.

The natural growth path leads then to the next stage, assuming nothing goes wrong in the process.

In the **conventional or ethnocentric/socio-centric stage,** the focus is on their core group. When a child grows up, more people enter its life and relationships shift. Now, there are other people to consider in order to survive, and the group takes on greater importance — the ME dynamic changes to a WE dynamic.

Other groups that might interfere with the surviving or thriving of one's group are considered bad or the enemy. In other words, the WE dynamic is an US versus THEM dynamic.

In most people's lives, the groups they belong to change, but not always the US versus THEM dynamic. For example, racial groups, religious groups, foreigners.

The natural growth path leads then to the next stage. However, many people get stuck in the ethnocentric stage because of internal or external life conditions which show, for example, as fears or adapting to group behavior.

In the **post-conventional or world-centric stage,** the focus shifts to all people on the planet. The US versus THEM dynamic becomes an all-encompassing WE dynamic. Differences between groups still exist, but they are not seen as a threat. The focus is on how everybody can live and work together.

To sum up the three main stages of consciousness development are: egocentric, socio-centric and world-centric.

As you might have guessed, there are benefits of a higher evolved consciousness:
- There are more options. When people are at a higher stage, they can go back to a lower one if a situation requires so. The other way around is not possible.
- One of the other major benefits of people who are at the world-centric stage is that their problem-solving capacity is exponentially higher.
- People at each next level are more compassionate. People who are in the world-centric stage are more compassionate than people in the socio-centric stage. People in the socio-centric stage are more compassionate than people in the egocentric stage.

At the same time, it is true that the more self-compassion a person has or, the more compassion they experience from their environment, the easier it is to develop from one stage to the next. Compassion is the means ànd result. That's why it's so important.

Since we are living in a global, interconnected world, we need more people that are at world-centric level. They have more options, have the more problem-solving capacity, and are more compassionate. It is at this world-centric level that full-grown Compassionate Leaders can be found.

When we link the three main levels of consciousness development to the four vibes, then we can conclude that:
- The highest vibe that someone in the egocentric stage can reach is the neutral vibe.
- The highest vibe that someone in the ethnocentric stage can reach is the positive vibe.
- To reach an inspiring vibe, someone needs to be in the world-centric stage.

That is why personal development that includes consciousness development is an often overlooked, but very important factor in raising the vibe of a team or organization. Later on in this chapter, you will be presented with a suggested approach: the Compassionate Leader Pathway.

The impact of different world views on an organization

When facilitating people in raising their vibe, but also in daily work, you are usually confronted with lots of discussions in your team, between departments and sometimes on a strategic level.

When you observe these discussions, you will notice a few things. Sometimes there can be discussions because people want to protect themselves (when they are in a negative or neutral vibe).

However, what puzzles most people is another phenomenon. You may notice that there are good intentions and a positive vibe at the beginning of a meeting, but that the vibe starts to spiral down after a while. People don't seem to understand each other or each other's arguments. This leads to frustration and interpersonal tensions. And it prevents constructive solutions that satisfy all involved parties.

The chances are that different participants look at the world from another perspective, without knowing it. When this happens, it is very hard to agree on a solution. Usually, this plays out more between different departments than in teams. The reason is that often people with the same world view are recruited by the manager of a team.

Usually, the three stages model (egocentric, socio-centric and world-centric) doesn't suffice to explain the differences and deal with them. One model with more subdivisions that provided me with deep insights is called Spiral Dynamics.

If you are familiar with the book *Spiral Dynamics* by Christopher Cowan and Don Beck or the Integral Theory model by Ken Wilber - that is also used by Frédéric Laloux in his book *Reinventing Organizations* - then you probably already made the link between the Yellow wave of Spiral Dynamics or the Teal level of Integral Theory and Compassionate Leadership.

Since *Spiral Dynamics* helped me a lot to become more compassionate, I wanted to include it in this book. But in the end, it didn't fit the flow of the book. So I created a separate e-book *The Compassionate Leader Explores Spiral Dynamics*.

So, I won't go into the details of those different world views in this book. However, I do want to share a few of my insights that are essential for organizations to deal with the complexity of today's world.

I already mentioned that there are a lot of great initiatives for creating a better workspace and increasing the vibe. Most of them are focused on *external* factors like software, technology, office design, or organizational structures.

The *internal* factors, like interpersonal and personal tensions, don't get that much attention. However, they are needed as much as the external ones.

Ken Wilber has created a model for those internal and external factors. He also explains why the internal factors don't receive much attention these days, why it is absolutely necessary to include them, and what is needed.

I present you a quick summary.

Ken Wilber's model is called AQAL: All Quadrants, All Levels. For now, let's focus on the 'All Quadrants' part.

Wilber makes a distinction between four quadrants in his AQAL model.

	Internal	External
Individual	**ME** Subjective Thoughts, emotions, memories, states of mind, perceptions and immediate sensations	**IT** Objective Material body (including brain), and anything you can see or touch (or observe scientifically) in time & space
Collective	**WE** Intersubjective Shared values, meaning, language, relationships and cultural background	**IT** Interobjective Systems, networks, technology, government and the natural environment

In the Internal-Individual quadrant (upper left), it's about what's going on inside a human being. It is about personal thoughts, feelings, emotions and sensations. They are described from the perspective of the first person: 'I'. In the External-Individual quadrant (upper right), it's about what you can see from the outside in terms of objective science. There you find neurotransmitters, a limbic system, molecules, DNA, organs and physical behavior. All of this is described in the third person: 'It'.

Each individual belongs to a group. That brings us to the Internal-Collective quadrant (lower left). The focus here is on aspects of the cultural realm: world view, shared values and relationships. This is described as 'We'. The External-Collective quadrant (lower right) contains group behavior, technological advancements and the environment. This is again described with 'It'.

What you will see, depends on the glasses (quadrant) you use. Concurrently you won't see the aspects that can be observed using other glasses. For example, when you look from the upper right quadrant (External-Individual), you can observe someone's behavior. You see person A yell at person B, and then you see person B leave. Why this person leaves and what happens inside them, can only be interpreted from the upper left quadrant. Maybe they got mad about what was said, maybe they got triggered by the way the message was communicated or maybe they were not affected at all, and they just had to leave for another appointment.

At this moment in time, the majority of business and political leaders looks rather unilaterally at the world: from the external quadrants (upper and lower right). Everything that can't be explained by science doesn't exist. As a consequence, according to them, the development of consciousness that takes place in the internal quadrants (upper and lower left) doesn't exist, although it was a crucial part in the development of science.

Why is this the leading view in the Western world at this moment? To find the answer, we need to go back in time.

The turning point was modernism. Before modernism, all quadrants were present, but also closely connected. Science and religion, for example, were inseparably linked to each other. A classic example is Galileo Galilei. The church fathers refused to look through his telescope because they claimed they already knew what was there to see.

Modernism gave way to the disconnection of the quadrants and further development, independent of each other. This has led to enormous progress!

However, what happened after a while is that the "It" quadrants evolved so fast that they started to dominate the other two. As a consequence, there was no room anymore for the "I" and "We" quadrants.

Modernism opened the way for technological advancements, material abundance, increased literacy and higher life expectancy. At the same time, lots of disadvantages came along as well: pollution, wastefulness, short-term thinking, and loss of meaning.

To develop further, an openness is needed and a willingness to look at all quadrants. In other words, no dominance of science and technology, but a balance with personal development and culture.

However, many techno-optimists and leaders of tech companies are not there yet. Only when they develop further, will technology be able to help humanity. Only when technology is balanced with what happens inside human beings, will real solutions be found.

One initiative, whose focus it is to open people's eyes and bring back humaneness, is the Center for Humane Technology (www.humatech.com). They are a team of deeply concerned former tech insiders who understand the culture, business incentives, design techniques, and organizational structures driving how technology hijacks our mind. On their website, they have several practical suggestions to transform the technology that steals our attention, to technology that supports our lives. This is a nice example of an initiative that doesn't want to destroy something but wants to increase awareness and consciousness to help tech companies improve.

Another trait of the external "It" quadrants from Wilber's model, is that they are extremely focused on economic growth. One of the consequences is that there aren't always enough studies done or enough cautionary measures taken. In my opinion, one of the examples is 5G. 5G is the fifth-generation cellular network that offers a huge boost in wireless speed. 5G is a technology that works on a much higher frequency. 1G, 2G, 3G, and 4G use between 1 to 6 gigahertz frequency. According to Kevin Mottus from the California Brain Tumor Association, 5G will use between 24 to 90 gigahertz frequency. Within the RF Radiation portion of the electromagnetic spectrum, the higher the frequency, the more dangerous it is to living organisms. 5G waves don't travel that far, so many new small masts need to be installed. That would be every 2 to 8 houses. Plus 20.000 5G satellites in space. In other words, lots of new sources of radiation, on top of the existing ones. It is still not clear what the effects on human beings, other living organisms and the planet will be. There are many organizations like the 5G appeal (www.5Gappeal.eu) that ask to postpone the rollout of 5G until its effects are clear. I fear that the radiation from 5G might have a huge impact on our brains and hence on our capacity for consciousness development. When not enough people can further develop their consciousness level, I don't see how we are going to be able to deal with global challenges. And even if the effect on humans is marginal, the effect on smaller creatures like bees might be much more impactful. Without bees, there won't be enough food for human beings, so it does impact humanity in the end. However, many tech companies and lobbying associations want to push 5G because of the technological advancements and potential economic growth it can bring. To me, this is a clear example of the dominance of the "It" quadrants over the "I" and "We" quadrants.

More insights in personal, organizational, and global development can be found in the e-book *The Compassionate Leader Explores Spiral Dynamics*.

Besides the focus on the external quadrants, there are other reasons why not all leaders are compassionate.

Why Aren't All Leaders Compassionate?

A remark I hear often is: "Aren't all leaders supposed to be compassionate, because of their role?" In theory, this is something you could expect, but reality shows something else. Let's investigate what the underlying cause is.

Growth in general and personal growth in particular, is a natural process. Compassion is also a natural state. However, things happen in our lives that distract us from this natural state. This happens to all human beings. Leaders are no exception.

There are three main causes why human beings, including leaders, are not always in a compassionate state. In other words, there are three main reasons why leaders are not Compassionate Leaders the whole time.

These reasons are:
1. There are too many distractions, too many situations and too many people that beg for their attention, including several that give them stress.
2. There are hidden differences between them and other people that create misunderstandings and keep them away from their strength.
3. There are protective patterns in their lives that keep them from being the most effective, efficient and inspiring leader they can be.

Let's dive a bit deeper into those three reasons.

Too many distractions

These days we are overloaded with information. Not only has the rate of information creation increased exponentially from 1960 till now, but also the number of media outlets has increased dramatically.

When you look up the knowledge information curve on the Internet, you will see that in 1900 knowledge doubled every century, in 1945 it was every 25 years, in 1982 every 12-13 months and, according to IBM, it will soon be every 12 hours.

In 1960, there were only newspapers, magazines, radio, and television. These days, websites and social media are added to the mix — plus the number of newspapers, magazines, radio stations, and television channels has increased tenfold. On top of that, we have more devices to consume information, and we can access them round-the-clock. Smartphones, e-mail, and social media have also changed our working habits. Many people can work anywhere, and almost all of us can be reached 24/7.

Besides that, most of us feel the need to have a vibrant social life to fit in with society. This creates extra stress, especially when rush-hour traffic on our way home becomes more and more unpredictable.

Information, work, commercials, and people are constantly asking for our attention. Then there are the attention-grabbing algorithms of social media, like Facebook, that are built in a way that makes it's hard to leave the site.

I call this phenomenon the *magnet of the rat race*. Because of devices and social media algorithms, it is a very powerful magnet and one that is always on.

The result is that most people feel that they don't have time for themselves. They don't have the time to flow in a natural way to their core stance or center. That's a pity since it's easier to be in touch with your compassionate state when you are centered.

Hidden differences between people

When people come from a different country, speak a different language or look a little different (like a man versus a woman or an adult versus a child), chances are higher that we give more attention to potential differences. However, when this is not the case, we often forget any differences.

As a consequence, misunderstandings and tensions can arise without us being aware of it. And our relationships suffer.

One of the examples of hidden differences involves different world views. For example, between the three main ones: egocentric, socio-centric or world-centric. It is clear that when people are approaching a challenge from different world views, without being aware of this difference, it is hard to find a solution. This can be very confusing, especially when there is no good communication model.

The result for many people is that they start conforming to others or start giving in to get out of endless discussions and get things done. However, they are not acting from their strength anymore.

Consequences can be that they get burnt out or lose joy in life. When we look at the scope of this book, it's harder to be compassionate for others if you don't have that feeling for yourself. This often creates a new tension that is discharged in interactions with other people. This leads to new interpersonal tensions which add an extra burden to the existing mix of tensions.

Protective patterns

Part of growing up as a human being is that you encounter smaller or larger physical and emotional pains, hurts and injuries.

Our body/mind has a mechanism to cope with these situations. It is the mechanism to cope with trauma.

But what is trauma exactly? Let's look at its definition.

According to the Oxford Dictionary, trauma is "a deeply distressing or disturbing experience" or "a physical injury." The origins of the word are Greek, meaning *wound*.

I refer to the definition because, for most people, trauma is something big like war experiences, a severe accident, sexual abuse, or mental torture.

But, as the definition shows, it can also be about smaller events. I prefer words like *hurts, injuries* or *pains* when it's about those smaller events, but the same principles apply.

However big or small the event, what happened is that a protective pattern is installed in an inner self. This pattern keeps us from reliving the emotions from the event. In other words, the pattern keeps us safe.

Those patterns serve us well, especially when we are kids and don't always have enough strength to take care of ourselves. As adults, it is a different case — many patterns we had as kids are not necessary anymore.

> Let's go back to the example of Danny. When Danny was a small boy, he was punished by his father for speaking when adults were having a conversation. After a while, he remained silent to avoid punishment. Being silent and not asking any questions became a survival strategy.

A protective pattern like this might harm us as adults or make us take irrational decisions.

> For example, when Danny graduated and was looking for a job, he had a hard time in interviews. He didn't ask any questions, so the interviewer assumed Danny wasn't interested. When he finally landed a job, he was overlooked for promotions despite his good work. The reason? He was silent in meetings and didn't ask any questions. He wasn't considered enthusiastic or engaged. This caused a high degree of frustration because Danny knew he had much more to offer. When he raised the topic with his manager, he was told to take a course to be more assertive. Although it helped a bit, it was still very hard for Danny to speak up. The reason was that he didn't realize that the cause of the problem was in his childhood. He also didn't realize that the assertiveness course only focused on the superficial layer instead of balancing his inner selves.

As you can see, those protective patterns keep us safe from getting harmed again, but at the same time, they limit our growth potential.

If we want to grow further, we need to start looking for the inner selves that are linked to those protective patterns. That is not always easy, because there is a fear connected to them. That fear keeps us from doing something that might harm us but also keeps us from balancing the inner selves that are involved. However, now that we know how this works, we can change our perspective. The pattern is not a fierce guardian that needs to keep us away *from*, but the pointer *towards* the place where an imbalance occurs.

Now that we have more clarity about the three reasons why most leaders are not compassionate yet let's look at how this can be changed using the Compassionate Leader Pathway.

The Compassionate Leader Pathway

Before we explore the Compassionate Leader Pathway, let's sum up what is needed to become a true Compassionate Leader.

These are the ingredients:
- Transforming the three reasons why leaders are not compassionate.
- Raising your compassion level.
- Knowing the techniques of the D.U.E.T. process so you can facilitate others.
- Balancing inner parts.
- Achieving the inspiring vibe.

As you can see, this can't be done in a one-hour session. It requires some kind of journey. It's like exercising. You don't build muscles in one workout.

So, to help leaders who want to become truly Compassionate Leaders, I have designed a pathway that includes all of the above ingredients.

What does the journey/pathway look like?

The three stages of the Compassionate Leader Pathway are:
- Weaken the Power of the Rat Race Magnet
- Improve Relationships
- Make Room for Growth

They each consist of three phases.

Why these stages? Because they answer the three main causes why most leaders are not compassionate all the time.

- We need to weaken the power of the rat race magnet to get more in our center and be less distracted.
- After discovering the hidden differences between other people and ourselves and after detecting our secure bases, combined with an effective communication model, we can operate from our strength instead of conforming ourselves. This leads to improved relationships.

- We need to balance our inner selves, so our protective patterns don't keep us from developing. The effect is that there is room for further growth.

The result? You will experience more freedom in your professional and personal life because you will be free from the distractions, preferences of others, and protective patterns. You will live in a higher permanent state of compassion. The consequence is that it will be much easier to cope with any situation that presents itself, no matter how tough it may seem at first.

This is what the Compassionate Leader Pathway looks like.

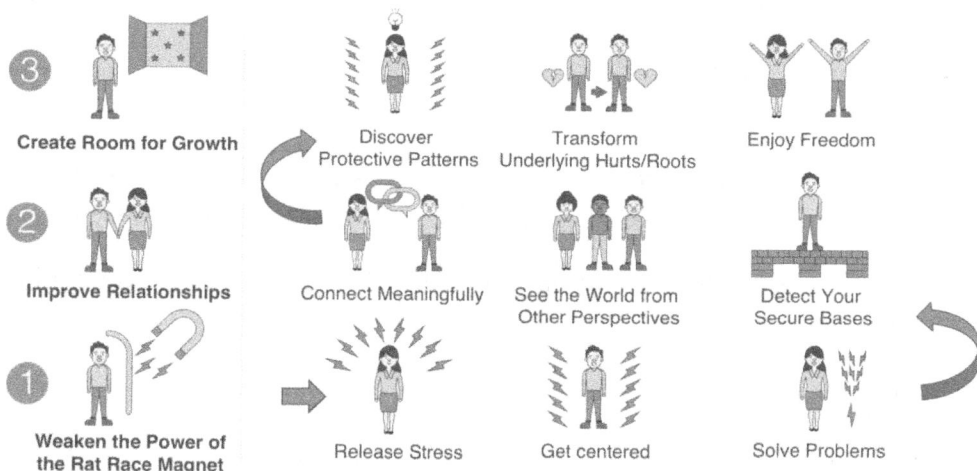

Let's look at the stages in more detail.

Stage 1: Weaken the Power of the Rat Race Magnet

Our complex and interconnected world is full of activity. It is like a magnet that has enormous power. It drags us into the treadmill of the rat race every day.

There are many ways to get into your center so you won't be distracted by the rat race. However, this is not easy — the reason: the *power* of the magnet. So, we need to weaken it.

What are the steps in this stage?

The first step is learning some simple **stress release methods**. The focus is on solving personal and interpersonal tensions. This creates more peacefulness and space for new insights and solutions.

Getting centered is the second step. This helps to stay in your strength, both in daily life, as in difficult moments like a meeting with a dissatisfied customer or when you have to share some bad news.

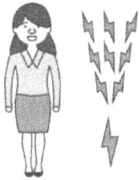

The third step is to **solve problems**. Usually, practical tension is ignored until it comes out via interpersonal tension. Then it is much harder to see which practical issue or process needs to be dealt with. That's why it is essential to be able to deal with practical or process tensions in a quick, harmonious and engaging way.

Is the magnet of the rat race gone after this stage? No, it hasn't and probably will never totally go away. It's kind of how the world works these days. However, its power over you will be weakened to a degree that you can start making other choices. Your feeling of freedom will already increase.

Stage 2: Improve Relationships

Nowadays, in this super-connected world, we can't get anything accomplished on our own anymore. We need to work with other people to reach our goals. This can mean working closely together on a full-time basis or less closely, on a project or freelance basis. Whatever the case, the best results stem from good relationships. That's why it is more important than ever before to stand in your power, detect differences between yourself and others, have ways to address them (so they won't get in the way of smoothly working together) and have an effective way of communicating.

In this second stage of the Compassionate Leader Pathway, the three steps are:

Detect Your Secure Bases. To be a secure base for someone else, you need to have secure bases yourself. They can be people, but also places, goals, or objects that provide a sense of protection, safety, and caring *and* offer a source of inspiration and energy for exploration, risk-taking and challenges. We all have them, but we are usually not aware of them. Remembering them gives you strength, makes it easier to be available for others (without having to dedicate much time) and is inspiring for your team members.

See the World from Other Perspectives. This helps to get insights into the roots of misunderstandings. This also helps to get the sting out of conflicts between team members or departments. As a result, openness emerges to find a solution constructively. Being able to detect the positive intentions behind (negative) behavior helps tremendously to improve relationships and the vibe in teams.

Connect Meaningfully. As a Compassionate Leader, it is important to listen to what is required by the people in your team, your organization, and the ecosystem. Often you will need to help them find their deeper need or concern, beyond their feelings or words. It is also important to voice your needs, or those of the team or organization you represent, in a clear way, so other people understand what you require.

Stage 3: Make Room for Growth

When we encounter hurts, injuries and blocks, growth can slow down or come to a halt, unless the underlying patterns are transformed.

It's not always easy to do this, though. It requires a willingness and courage to look at the behavior that is deemed negative by others or ourselves: the excesses of our primary or disowned selves.

Courage and willingness are essential. That's why the first two stages of the Compassionate Leader Pathway are so important. In the first stage, you learn to weaken the power of the rat race magnet, so you are less distracted and triggered. In the second stage, you learn to appreciate the differences between people and learn to notice which gifts for self-discovery they bring you.

The goal of the first two stages is twofold: to have you go through the experience of those stages and learn to apply the associated techniques from the D.U.E.T. process on the one hand and to prepare for the third stage on the other. Since your compassion level has risen after the first two stages, it is now much easier to look at negative behavior as a pointer to the real cause than it was at the beginning of the first stage.

The main invitation in this third stage is to look at your shadow sides as the pointer to where imbalances between inner selves reside.

When you are aware of how this process works, you can detect for yourself or for people you work or live with where there is behavior that might be a pointer to events that keep you, or others stuck. Just noticing this and avoiding being sucked up in the wave of emotions caused by the primary or disowned selves, will already make you a more Compassionate Leader.
The steps in this third stage of the Compassionate Leader Pathway are:

Discover Protective Patterns. In this first step, it is about discovering patterns that were once necessary, but not anymore. It is about finding imbalances between inner selves. This is an important step because we can only change what we are aware of.

Transform Underlying Hurts/Roots. Once you have discovered where the imbalances between inner selves are situated, you can start transforming and healing the underlying causes. Sometimes they are about hurts from the past; sometimes, they have more neutral roots. Transforming the imbalances releases energy that can help you to reach your goals faster and with less effort.

Enjoy Freedom. Once you have balanced the inner selves, more room for growth is available. Actually, you have created more space for the natural growth process. By now, you have also become a Compassionate Leader. This gives so much more freedom. You won't be as distracted anymore. You will see the roots of tensions sooner and more clearly. You will be able to help solve tensions and probably even balance inner selves in your team and in the organization. As a result, everybody in the organization and the organization itself can continue to grow. And who knows, maybe other Compassionate Leaders will arise because of your example.

To support leaders and facilitators to become true Compassionate Leaders, I have created the Raise the Vibe program, based on this Compassionate Leader Pathway.

There is an online and live version of the Raise the Vibe program available. The online program is designed as short modules for leaders and facilitators who don't have much time. The extras of the live program are: practicing the techniques, balancing inner parts with a coach and making deep connections with fellow Compassionate Leaders. You can find the details on the website.

Habits of a Compassionate Leader

As a way of summarizing the most important insights and take-aways from this book, let's describe the actions and habits of Compassionate Leaders who raised their Compassionate Leadership level by following the Compassionate Leader Pathway and who use the tools from the D.U.E.T. process to facilitate their team(s).

Compassionate Leaders know that there are four vibes: negative, neutral, positive, and inspiring. Each higher vibe than the negative one is characterized by higher performance, higher problem-solving capacities, better collaboration, more well-being, and greater attractiveness for top talent. Each vibe lower than the inspiring one comes with a cost: people spend more time protecting themselves from potential (psychological) danger, projects slow down, performance decreases, co-workers are less available due to illnesses, and top talent may leave the team or company.

Compassionate Leaders know that vibes fluctuate and that people adapt to the vibe of the group. To get the centers of gravity to a higher level, a deliberate effort is usually needed: transforming tensions by using techniques like the ones from the D.U.E.T. framework. This is only possible when the vibe of the leader allows it. He or she needs to transform their vibe first before there is space for the team or organization.

Compassionate Leaders know that each vibe and each transition to a higher vibe needs a different approach. Vibes are the easiest to recognize when tensions show up. This can be in day-to-day work or in change projects. There are three different types of tension: practical or process tension, personal tension, and interpersonal tension.

In organizations, most tensions are related to practical or personal tensions. However, if they are not dealt with, interpersonal tensions are easily created and added to the mix. This usually leads to a temporary or permanent decrease in vibe. That's why Compassionate Leaders apply techniques like the ones from the D.U.E.T. framework.

When it's about the word *compassion* there are two key insights. The first is that there is a distinction between suffering and pain. The second is that the translation of the word compassion is *be with pain or suffering* instead of *suffer with*. This makes a huge difference in being compassionate in the workplace (and at home).

For Compassionate Leaders, compassion means being able to be with some-one, even if they are having a hard time or behaving negatively, without suffering themselves. It is about seeing them as a fellow, equivalent human being, instead of a victim. It is about being able to keep a focus on their talents and positive qualities while allowing the pain to be expressed.

This doesn't mean tolerating negative behavior. It means noticing the behav-ior and knowing that this is a way of getting rid of tension. Being compassion-ate is being able first to allow the tension to be expressed in a non-destructive way, and then discover and, if possible, transform the root of the tension. It's about knowing that the tension that is experienced is the pointer to what it's really about.

For Compassionate Leaders, being compassionate means supporting the other person to get out of victim mode (if they were in it) and helping them to see other options. For Compassionate Leaders, it is about staying in their own center, in their own power, and not being sucked into another person's ener-gy. It's about connecting with the other person, without getting caught up in their feelings or emotions. This allows them to be able to keep seeing extra or new options.

They look at resistance in general and resistance to change in particular as signs that something important is on the verge of being forgotten, ignored, or cut out. Compassionate Leaders welcome resistance as another form of tension and consider it as an opportunity to grow. This opportunity can be on the level of the organization, a team, or an individual. Compassionate Leaders consider all levels important.

The definition of Compassionate Leadership helps them to stay focused: "The ability to take individuals, teams, and organizations to a higher vibe, meaning a higher level of performance and well-being, in a safe and stimulating way when tensions occur."

Compassionate Leaders welcome tension. They consider tension as an indica-tor of opportunities for growth. They use it as a pointer to go to the root and transform the underlying cause or patterns. They 'navigate by tension' to increase the results and well-being of their team. They use the D.U.E.T. framework as their toolkit to reach this goal and increase the vibe at the same time.

They also keep the bonding cycle in mind whenever any type of change happens: first the stage of attachment (which provides some comfort), then the stage of bonding (which strength is defined by the level of interest put in the relationship), then the stage of separation (which prepares us for the new situation beyond grief) and the final stage of grieving (which allows us to expand our identity and embrace our future self).

Compassionate Leaders know that they have a large impact on their team. If they want to support others, they need to be a secure base for them. It is hard to be one if they don't know their own secure bases. That's why they make time to detect and list them.

They are sensitive to perpetrator-victim relationships and also rescuer-victim relationships. If necessary, they use the Compassion Technique when they recognize what is going on. And then they use the Compassion Quadrants and the Inner Balance Technique to find out to which inner selves the struggle with the other person is pointing and then balance them.

Compassionate Leaders are sensitive to judging and projection as well. If they become aware of someone judging or projecting their situation on them or vice versa, they use the Compassion Technique to get back in their center and make the relationship equal again. Then they use the Compassion Quadrants to find out which inner selves are at play. Once they are discovered, they use the Inner Balance Technique to balance them.

Compassionate Leaders avoid unsolicited advice. They ask for permission first. If they are facilitating a meeting, they ensure that the participants only give their opinion or advice when requested. Sometimes they use a talking stick to facilitate this process.

In other words, Compassionate Leaders use the techniques from the D.U.E.T. process to turn the strategies of the ego around. The more they do this, the less powerful those strategies are, and the less frequent they will show up. As a consequence, it is easier to be or remain compassionate.

Compassionate Leaders hold the space for others. Together with a compassionate attitude, this might be enough for the other person to get going again. If the other person needs their help, they don't come up with solutions right away. They ask permission first. If the other person is open to it, Compassionate Leaders go through the D.U.E.T. process with them. They have experienced that facilitating a team member can be very liberating. They don't have to do anything except follow the instructions. This is an easy step towards being present and holding the space for others.

Compassionate Leaders understand that there are a lot of hidden dynamics behind tensions. They are aware that those hidden dynamics can be at play whenever they can't put their finger on the tension that shows itself. They have an open mind and a compassionate curiosity to discover what is going on, instead of assuming they already know the underlying cause.

Compassionate Leaders know and apply the D.U.E.T. framework. They use the Compassion Technique to solve interpersonal tension, The ABCs of De-stressing for personal tension and Compassionate Problem Solving for practical tension. If the situation requires it, Compassionate Leaders then go to the next phase in the D.U.E.T. process: they facilitate the other person to embrace and transform the root of the tension. They use Compassion Quadrants for interpersonal tension, the Inner Balance Technique for personal tension and, if necessary, Compassionate Problem Solving again for practical tension. Then the last step can be taken: the proposal that was formed in Compassionate Problem Solving can be applied, some action for self-care can be taken, or a conversation can be started using Compassionate Communication. They also are aware that the D.U.E.T. framework offers flexibility. If it's not the right time to go through steps 2 and 3, they can immediately apply Compassionate Communication (step 4) after having detected a tension (step 1).

Compassionate Leaders know that an extra benefit of knowing and using the D.U.E.T. process is having a reference frame and a common language. For example, when every team member knows the Compassion Quadrants technique, the leader might say: "I notice you keep having conflicts with the marketing department. Why don't we use the Compassion Quadrants to find out what it's really about." Or before or during a meeting, the leader can say: "We all know this is a rather delicate subject. Let's all do the Compassion Technique first." The benefit is that there is less blaming, less defensiveness, more openness, faster transforming of tensions, and quicker raising of the vibe.

When the other person is showing negative behavior or when Compassionate Leaders feel resistance or tension with regard to the other person, they keep in mind that it is just a primary or disowned self that is playing out, that all the other parts are NOT showing negative behavior and that there is an imbalance between a primary and disowned self.

Compassionate Leaders realize words have an impact. That's why they deliberately choose their words. A first way is to use neutral words. For example, they use the word *tension* instead of *problem*. They know that the word *but* erases everything before it in a sentence. For example: "I like your detailed analysis, but let's ask Kevin's opinion." They deliberately change the word *but* to *and* use this sentence only when they mean it. They also know how destructive the phrase "Yes, but ..." can be for a constructive dialogue. So, they refrain from using it, similar to war-like words and exaggerations. They also replace the words *should, ought, must,* and *need* with *choose*.

These words are a part of Compassionate Communication, together with a compassionate attitude, having an open mind, and focusing on clarity. If necessary, Compassionate Leaders use the four-step structure when speaking or listening. In general, those steps are:
- State the objective facts or what you have observed.
- Share or check the emotions around the facts or observation.
- Explore the needs or concerns behind the emotions.
- Formulate a request.

Compassionate Leaders offer a safe space for their team(s). In that space, operational, organizational tensions can easily be processed. The same space also offers a safe place for personal or interpersonal tensions to be healed or transformed. In that way, harmonious and high performing teams are created.

They take the long-term potential of each team member into account. In the negative vibe, this helps them stay in a compassionate mode. From the neutral vibe on, they voice this potential to their team members to give them a secure and inspiring future image of themselves.

When their team members feel powerless because they have the feeling they do not influence decisions that impact them, Compassionate Leaders show them which factors they *can* influence. They also share the why and the bigger picture behind decisions with their team.

Compassionate Leaders know how important it is to be a role model for every transition. The most challenging transition for leaders is usually the one towards the inspiring vibe. This requires a lot of vulnerability and a willingness to discover blind spots and explore shadow sides.

However, since they understand that shadows give shelter to disowned selves and since they know that embracing these disowned selves will benefit them tremendously, this is not something to be fearful of anymore. On the contrary, Compassionate Leaders welcome opportunities to balance their inner selves. Compassionate Leaders know that they are a huge factor with regards to the vibe of their team or organization. In order not to limit their team members, they choose the path of self-development and deep inner work.

Compassionate Leaders look for ways to develop themselves because it provides them with more options. They know that protective patterns limit their natural growth. As a result, they welcome situations where those protective patterns show up, both positively and negatively. They are vulnerable because they know it's the easiest way to detect and face tensions. If necessary, they use the D.U.E.T. process. They also know that these principles don't only apply to them, but also to their team members and the rest of the organization.

They consider themselves facilitators and midwives of this continuous growth process. They know that facing tension might be frightening, but they also know that the pain of the fear is bigger than the actual pain of transforming the root of the tension. Usually there is actually no pain, but a feeling of relief since more energy becomes available.

Compassionate Leaders have the ambition of taking their team or organization into an inspiring vibe. They know it is a journey. They celebrate success when a higher vibe is reached. They don't judge themselves or their team on not being in the inspiring vibe yet but have a compassionate look at their situation.

Compassionate Leaders know the three major stages of consciousness development: egocentric, socio-centric/ethnocentric, and world-centric. They understand that to face today's global challenges the world-centric stage is the most beneficial.

They are aware of the fact that true Compassionate Leaders have evolved towards this world-centric stage. They know that personal development programs, based on frameworks like the Compassionate Leader Pathway, support reaching the world-centric stage. And that they help in creating the space for the inspiring vibe for everyone.

Gizmo Objects Inc.

You are probably wondering how Catherine, Frank and all the other employees of Gizmo Objects Inc. are doing. To conclude this book, let's see what happened to them. Let's start with Catherine and the customer service department.

A year and a half after Catherine replaced Hans as manager of the customer service department, a complete shift has happened. Where the team had its center of gravity in the negative vibe a year ago, now it has entered the early phase of the inspiring vibe.

People from other departments can't believe what they see when they visit the offices of the customer service department. A year and a half ago, everybody avoided the area because of the toxic atmosphere. Now, people hop in for a quick visit to be refreshed by its cheerful mood.

Absenteeism due to sick leave has decreased dramatically, and team members are helping each other out whenever they can. Performance has steadily increased over the past eight months, along with double-digit growth in solving customer complaint cases.

While Catherine was first needed as a kind of shelter from the storm, her role transformed into being a coach for team members. Once the team was ready for it, Catherine asked for more options to support them in their personal growth. Because her progress didn't go unnoticed by CEO John and COO Helen, Catherine was granted a budget to do this. Catherine used those funds for both group training and external personal coaching. This has been proven very fruitful. Team members are now learning how to become coaches for each other (peer-to-peer coaching).

Being able to coach each other is important for the next step for the team because they want to be a self-managing team. The team has many other plans as well. They are working on a proposal to use a different customer complaint handling system. If everything goes well, they will be able to present it to John and Helen next month. Since the idea and the research came from the team itself, Catherine will only be attending the meeting for moral support.

The customer service team also has been looking into how they could implement other ways of working together like Holacracy and Sociocracy 3.0. They know that it's currently a bridge too far for Gizmo Objects Inc. because John and Helen haven't made transitioning to the inspiring vibe a priority for the whole company yet. However, the customer service team doesn't want to be held back by that and is keen to explore which elements of those inspiring examples they can already use at a team level.

Although John and Helen haven't emphasized supporting the whole company to raise its vibe, they have been following up on developments in the customer service department firmly since the moment Catherine was able to take the team quickly to the neutral vibe. They have also been keeping an eye on what the R&D team has been doing. In the past, they thought that its ability to work in the inspiring vibe was because of the nature of R&D work and the university degrees of its team members. But because of Catherine's success with the customer service department, John and Helen are now more interested in what is possible for the rest of the organization.

While John and Helen are still contemplating what to do, other teams have not been waiting. After marketing manager George experienced the power of Compassionate Problem Solving first hand, he asked Catherine if she could assist the marketing team in using this technique as well. She had explained to him that it was part of the D.U.E.T. framework. She had also pointed out to him that it is necessary to take the different vibes into account. Since George didn't want to follow a training course to learn the model and how to facilitate it, he had asked Catherine if she could support his team.

Catherine had accepted this challenge. She had considered it as an excellent opportunity to work more with the D.U.E.T. framework. Besides, since her team was performing better week after week, she wasn't needed as much. So, she had time to support the marketing team.

Facilitating George's team had been a very rewarding experience for Catherine. She had noticed how her self-confidence to facilitate others had grown, together with her insights in human behavior and the dynamics between people. She not only loves to facilitate others using the D.U.E.T. framework, but she loves to share her experiences and insights with others as well.

When Catherine's team reached the early stage of the inspiring vibe, it was clear that it wouldn't stop there. The potential of a true self-managing team was present. Catherine knew that she still might be useful as a soundboard, but most of her added value would be taken over by the team after a while. So, she already started designing another role for herself besides being the manager of the customer service department. She was keen on being a facilitator of the D.U.E.T. framework for other teams and a speaker at events to share her insights about the vibes. When she presented her new roles to John and Helen, they gladly accepted her proposal. They were happy that they wouldn't lose this talented employee and saw the value she could bring to the rest of her company in her new role.

You might wonder what happened to the other protagonists of Gizmo Objects Inc. Well, let's take a look at them.

Catherine was able to keep Ariane on board in the beginning when everybody went to the neutral vibe. However, the next steps went too fast for Ariane, and she decided to ask for a transfer to another team. This was granted.

Hans was able to recover from burnout after a year. However, in that process, he had learned that he wasn't excited about being a manager. He liked the title and the benefits but didn't feel very fulfilled. Before being the manager of the customer service department, he had worked in the accounting department, where he had become the manager. Hans now realized he liked working with numbers and that he missed the work. So, he decided to focus his abilities in that direction again. However, going back to Gizmo Objects Inc. and working as a regular team member in the accounting department made him feel like a bit of a failure. One of his inner parts was not ready to deal with what felt like a big demotion. After he found the courage to tell this to John and Helen, they helped him find a job in another company where he could make a fresh start.

The person who had experienced the biggest turnaround was Frank. From being stuck in a negative vibe, he had become the one who was on the forefront of learning new tools and techniques. Catherine had played a big role in this. She had been a secure base for him. When Frank looked back, it was all that he needed, together with the D.U.E.T. framework. He had experienced that when he could stand on this foundation, it was rather easy to deal with all the challenges that came up. He had been able to show his potential to the team and the rest of the organization. John and Helen had been notified of his pioneering role. They had seen the potential of a manager in him, but Catherine had warned them to look out for the Peter Principle: in hierarchic systems, people tend to be promoted until they reach a level of incompetence. So, instead of promoting him into a management function, John and Helen talked to Frank about how he saw his future role. Frank had told him that he loved being on the phone with customers and finding solutions for their problems. He had also told them that he thought he would perform at his best in a self-managing team: he would be able to combine his expert and leadership skills while still being in touch with customers. Since that was the way the customer service department was heading anyway, John and Helen decided not to change anything. Much to Frank's delight!

Next Steps

If you are like me, you have read the book from start to finish but didn't take the time to go to the website to access the extra resources or join the Compassionate Leaders community where you can connect with like-minded people.

So, the next step could be to do that now and create a free account on the website of The Compassionate Leader: www.thecompassionateleader.org

This account allows you to:

- **Become a member of the community** where you can find other (aspiring) Compassionate Leaders from all over the world. It is a great place to find like-minded leaders and facilitators; and to read and share articles and best practices about applying compassion in the workplace, experiences with the D.U.E.T. framework and being or becoming a Compassionate Leader.

- **Access the Training Center that includes:**
    o A free section with various exercises, resources, and tools including:
        - Exercise to find secure bases.
        - The visual of the D.U.E.T. process.
        - The Compassion Technique video.
        - Instructions of the Compassion Technique in PDF.
        - A link to the ABCs of De-stressing video.
        - Instructions of the Compassion Quadrants in PDF.
        - Examples of Compassion Quadrants.
        - Lists with emotions and needs for the four-step structure of Compassionate Communication.
    o Premium section which includes several resources and courses including:
        - The *Compassionate Leader Explores Spiral Dynamics* e-book.
        - Raise the Vibe Programs (which follow the steps of the Compassionate Leader Pathway).

- Easily register for one of the **webinars or live events** where you can meet other members or practice the Compassion Technique, Compassion Quadrants, Compassionate Communication, or one of the other techniques of the D.U.E.T. process.

I look forward to meeting you in the community!

Jan

For Organizations

Jan and other members of the Compassionate Leader team are available as speakers, as workshop and program facilitators, and as coaches.

These are a few examples of formats and topics:

- Keynote presentations.
    - How to create the space for an inspiring vibe.
    - The three stages of becoming a Compassionate Leader.
    - How to transform tension into growth.
    - What will we teach A.I.?
    - Compassionate Leadership: a must-have for self-managing teams.
    - How compassion boosts innovation.
- Workshops about one or more of the techniques of the D.U.E.T. process.
- A dedicated team program focused on which transition your team needs to make (negative to the neutral vibe, neutral to the positive vibe, positive to inspiring vibe).
- The Raise the Vibe programs for leaders and facilitators which follows the Compassionate Leader Pathway.

Contact us via connect@thecompassionateleader.org if you would like us to contribute to your personal or organizational growth or fulfilling your personal purpose or that of your company.

Acknowledgments

On this page, I want to thank all the people on whose shoulders I could stand in making this book a reality. They have been sources of inspiration, secure bases, and examples of what it's like to be a Compassionate Leader or to aspire to be one.

My deepest gratitude goes to my wife Gwendolyn. There is the usual appreciation that any author has for moral support, taking over practical chores, and having to spend a lot of time without them during the writing process. In my case, she has been much more than that. She has been a major soundboard for ideas and a guinea pig for the new techniques I developed. My dearest *super wife*, many, many thanks for all the hours of discussing the concepts, giving 'feedforward' and of course, our profound systemic/constellation work together. Thank you for all your support, especially in the times when I got stuck finding and fitting the pieces into the puzzle. My personal journey hasn't been easy either, in making the transition from my previous company, Networking Coach to the Compassionate Leader. Thanks for standing by my side!

If I were to list all the authors that have been an inspiration in my life so far and that have consciously or unconsciously contributed to this book, it would cover endless pages. You can find a small selection in the Sources and Recommended Literature section. However, in particular, I want to mention the authors whose work is part of the foundation for the D.U.E.T. framework: Marina Riemslagh, Daniel Ofman, Hal & Sidra Stone, Marshall Rosenberg, James Priest, Bernhard Bockelbrink and Liliana David. Also special thanks to George Kohlrieser, Susan Goldsworthy, Duncan Coombe, Robert Kegan, Lisa Laskow Lahey, Ray Dalio, Kristin Neff, Daniel Pink, Brian Robertson and Ken Wilber for their great ideas and concepts that I have mentioned throughout the book.

I'm also very grateful for the people who have extensively reviewed the book during the writing process: Philippe Bailleur, Emiel De Schepper, Ives De Saeger, Frédérique Michiels, Jan Beyen, Peter Plusquin, Jef Cumps, and Anja Moortgat. You have time and again challenged my ideas, the structure of the book, and the connections between concepts. You inspired me with your ideas and suggestions of books and resources to check out. Thanks to you, the book has reached not one, but several higher levels!

I want to express my appreciation to all our corporate customers and personal clients. Thanks for trusting me in the process and being open for experiments. This helped me to test my ideas and techniques and bring them to their current state.

My gratitude also goes to Jeff Hurst and Janet William who edited the English version. Thanks for correcting my non-native English and simplifying the construction of the sentences. You have made the book an easier read!

Sources and Recommended Literature

Bailleur, Philippe. *Stuck? Dealing with organizational trauma.*

Baert Ann. *Van Binnen Uit. Vijf stappen naar versnelde en duurzame groei.*

Barrett, Richard. *Liberating the Corporate Soul.*

Beck, Don en Cowan, Chris. *Spiral Dynamics. Mastering Values, Leadership and Change.*

Callens, Joost. *De Kwetsbare Leider. Bouwstenen voor persoonlijke ontwikkeling en leiderschap.*

Chapman Gary. *The 5 languages of appreciation in the workplace.*

Chapman Gary. *The 5 love languages.*

Cumps Jef. *Sociocratie 3.0.*

Dalio Ray. *Principles.*

De Blot, Paul. *Business Spiritualiteit. Een vernieuwingsmodel voor organisaties in een crisis.*

De Blot, Paul. *De mystiek van het zakendoen. Op zoek naar de spirituele kracht van organisaties.*

Kegan, Robert and Laskow Lahey, Lisa. *An Everyone Culture.*

Koenders Erik en Nientied Peter. *De menskant van veranderen. Spiral Dynamics in de praktijk.*

Kohlrieser George, Goldsworthy Susan and Coombe Duncan. *Care to Dare.*

Kübler-Ross Elisabeth en Kessler, David. *On Grief and Grieving: Finding the Meaning of Grief Through the Five Stages of Loss.*

Laloux, Frederic. *Reinventing Organizations.*

Neff, Kristin. *Self Compassion.*

Ofman, Daniel. *Building Commitment and Enthusiasm in Organizations.*

Ofman, Daniel. *Fancy meeting me here.*

Oostvogels, Kim. *Zeal.*

Priest, James, Bockelbrink, Bernhard and David, Liliana. *Sociocracy 3.0, a practical guide.*

Pink, Daniel. *A whole new mind. Why right brainers will rule the future.*

Pink, Daniel. *Drive. The surprising truth about what motivates us.*

Riemslagh, Marina. *Stop Stress, Create Your Life. How to Resolve the Effects of Stress.*

Rosenberg, Marshall. *Nonviolent Communication: A Language of Life.*

Robertson Brian. *Holacracy.*

Ruppert Franz. *Trauma, Bonding & Family Constellations: Understanding and Healing Injuries of the Soul.*

's Jongers Peter. *Trots!*

Scharmer, Otto. *Theory U: Leading from the Future as It Emerges.*

Semler Ricardo. *Maverick: The Success Story Behind the World's Most Unusual Workplace.*

Stam, Jan Jacob. *Fields of Connection.*

Stam, Jan Jacob. *Wings for change.*

Stone Hal & Sidra. *Embracing Ourselves.*

Torfs, Wouter. *Werken met Hart en Ziel. Bouwstenen voor een Great Place to Work.*

Van Reybrouck David en D'Ansembourg Thomas. *Vrede kun je leren.*

Vermeiren, Jan. *Life is a Game! Keys for a light and purposeful life full of Joy.*

Wilber Ken. *Integral Psychology. Consciousness, spirit, psychology, therapy.*

Wilber Ken. *A Theory of Everything. An integral vision for business, politics, science and spirituality.*

Worline, Monica and Dutton, Jane, *Awakening Compassion At Work.*

The Author: Jan Vermeiren

Jan Vermeiren (1974) is the founder of The Compassionate Leader.

The mission of The Compassionate Leader is: creating the space for an inspiring vibe.

Jan is the author of two international best sellers about online/offline networking: *Let's Connect!* and *How to REALLY use LinkedIn*. He is also the author of *Life is a Game!* (which focuses on personal and spiritual development) and co-author of five other books.

Jan and the teams in his previous company, Networking Coach, and current company, The Compassionate Leader, have worked for more than 500 organizations all over the globe including Alcatel, Deloitte, IBM, ING, Nike, Orange, Philips, Rabobank, Siemens and several Chambers of Commerce.

One of the achievements that Jan is still very proud of is that Networking Coach was the first training company in the world that was certified by LinkedIn.

Jan has been a guest lecturer at several universities and business schools, including the international MBA programs of Vlerick Business School (Belgium) and Rotterdam School of Management (the Netherlands). According to HR Tribune, he is one of the top 10 speakers in his home country Belgium.

Jan lives in Lier with Gwendolyn and her two sons, Elias and Jonathan. His current hobbies are dance theater, Taiko and watching basketball (after 21 years playing himself).

www.ingramcontent.com/pod-product-compliance
Lightning Source LLC
Chambersburg PA
CBHW051753200326

41597CB00025B/4539